Top 10
United Methodist
Beliefs

Top
10
United
Methodist
Beliefs

Don Adams
Foreword by
Bishop Michael Watson

Abingdon Press
Nashville

TOP 10 UNITED METHODIST BELIEFS

Copyright © 2016 by Abingdon Press

This book is printed on acid-free paper.

Library of Congress Cataloging-in-Publication Data

Names: Adams, Donald L. (Pastor)
Title: Top 10 United Methodist beliefs / Don Adams ; foreword by Bishop
   Michael Watson.
Other titles: Top ten United Methodist beliefs
Description: Nashville, Tennessee : Abingdon Press, 2016. | Includes
   bibliographical references and index.
Identifiers: LCCN 2015035593 (print) | LCCN 2015036340 (ebook) | ISBN
   9781501804229 (binding: pbk.) | ISBN 9781501804236 (e-pub)
Subjects: LCSH: United Methodist Church (U.S.)—Doctrines. | Wesley, John,
   1703-1791.
Classification: LCC BX8331.3 .A33 2016 (print) | LCC BX8331.3 (ebook) | DDC
   230/.7—dc23
LC record available at http://lccn.loc.gov/2015035593

16 17 18 19 20 21 22 23 24 25—10 9 8 7 6 5 4 3 2 1
MANUFACTURED IN THE UNITED STATES OF AMERICA

Contents

Contents

Acknowledgments

The production of a book such as this truly takes a village. I am indebted to the staff at Abingdon Press, especially Kathy Armistead, David Teel, and Laura Wheeler for their highly professional and always gracious guidance and support. Too, I am deeply thankful for the remarkable work of the many Wesley scholars I have referred to in this material.

My wife, Brenda, is a person who seeks to live a life of holy love. Her encouragement along with the love and prayerful support of my children and their families was instrumental in keeping this project moving forward. Once for a contemporary worship service I had a T-shirt printed that said, "I Am the Most Blessed Person You Know." Thanks be to God from whom every blessing ultimately flows!

Foreword

John Wesley's powerful impact on the history of the world's understanding of humanity and God, and the relationship between humanity and God, is worthy of thoughtful consideration by people everywhere. Don Adams has written a book that is most helpful to that thoughtful consideration. All who read this very clear presentation of John Wesley's understanding and proclamation of God's amazing love will have an increased appreciation for how we are challenged to celebrate divine love and become more faithful disciples of Jesus Christ, who is the incarnation of God's grace, for the transformation of the world.

This book is a wonderful resource for individuals and congregations who are open to learning more about what it means to think, believe, and live in the Wesleyan tradition. It is honest and thought-provoking. It opens the reader to an exciting adventure into the mind of a Christian disciple whose remarkable life embodied holy living in an age of global upheaval. It offers a pathway for today's Christian believers to mature in faithful living during this age of global commotion even as Wesley did in his day.

Don Adams is a gifted minister of the gospel of Jesus Christ whose deepest desire is to grow in grace and help others to do the same. While serving as his bishop, and because of my great respect for him, I asked him to become a spiritual guide to pastors and lay people as the super-intendent of an entire district of local churches and ministries. I am grateful for the opportunities that the resulting shared ministry gave me to benefit from his thoroughly Wesleyan approach to Christian faith. The readers of this book will benefit from that same pastoral theology put into print.

Don has studied John Wesley. He has taught Wesleyan studies. He has lived the Wesleyan way. He has even brought the father of the Methodist movement to life as an actor who is regularly asked to portray John Wesley for audiences far and wide. Many who see Don, see John. This book is yet another way for Don Adams to help us see that John Wesley's dynamic Christian faith remains vitality relevant today.

Michael Watson
Resident Bishop
North Georgia Episcopal Area
The United Methodist ChurchSomeone

Introduction

Before You Begin: Put On the Wesley Lenses

Are you satisfied with shallow, simplistic salvation? John Wesley was not.

On many occasions as the jailer's cart rolled with its condemned passenger toward the gallows, John or his brother, Charles, would hop into the wagon for one last appeal. They were not above a simple presentation of the offer of forgiveness to someone whose future could be measured in minutes. Is that a sufficient understanding of the gospel for you?

Unless life could be measured in minutes, it wasn't for Wesley. His study of scripture had convinced him that God's plan in sending his Son into the world was much richer and deeper than forgiveness alone. God's plan was Christlikeness, powerfully pure motives, and fruitfully mature graces. Christ came so ocean-deep, holy love could transform human lives into persons of notable character and courage—the image of God clearly in the process of being restored.

Recently I attended a change-of-command ceremony where my friend and engaged Christian marine Major General Jim Kessler was being reassigned. While the program was one of high ritual, just beneath the spit and polish of it all was the reality that these were warriors. Beyond the ceremonial pomp were issues of life and death. I found myself thinking about how easily the church grows numb to the battle beyond our ceremonies. John Wesley refused to be content with ceremony-deep religion. There is a battle at hand that only holy warriors will have the wherewithal to fight and win.

Year in and year out, those in Wesley's Methodist gatherings had responded to the great invitation to trust in Jesus. They were then wholeheartedly exhorted to *continue* through participation in Methodist societies, class meetings, and bands. These incubators of scriptural piety were joined with the expectation of works of mercy, engaging the rough-edged needs of a fallen world. What was at stake was not some kind of divine insurance policy. What was in the balance, as New Testament scholar N. T. Wright would phrase it, was God in Christ "putting the world to rights."[1]

Working out our part in God's plan is a battle. Part of the battle is right living, and part of the battle is right believing.

Working out our part in God's plan is a battle. Part of the battle is right living, and part of the battle is right believing. For Wesley, right believing was crucial in winning the battle. He fought vigorously to overcome the obstacles to clear thinking, growth in grace, and obedience. The idea of a spiritually satisfied Methodist was, for Wesley, a contradictory concept. The Methodist/Wesleyan tradition is truly a call to transformation.

There is no debate about what Jesus considered "the main thing." The so-called Great Commandment, Matthew 22:37-38, to love God with all of our heart and soul and mind, and its immediate partner commandment, to love one's neighbor, are the nonnegotiable priorities Jesus established. Wesley's first priority was growing Christian disciples whose default heart setting is the kind of holy love longing to keep these commandments. We're talking about raising up warriors for the "good fight" (2 Tim 4:7) where the struggle is always in service to love.

Top 10 Methodist Beliefs is not intended to resolve all of the differences in the definition of right living. This material has been written in an effort to help Christian people give meaningful consideration to how one of history's most significant Christian leaders, John Wesley, proclaimed and defended the sort of right thinking that produced disciples who fought the good fight. He clearly understood that orthodoxy (right thinking) is a means and not an end. Right doing is the goal. But he also clearly understood that wrong thinking only accidentally leads to right living. Satan, the adversary, is identified as a liar in John 8:44, implying that the essence of evil is untruth. Therefore the most characteristic temptation of evil is the invitation to believe what is not true or what is only half true. Followers of Jesus Christ are in a battle to live in the truth as it was in Christ Jesus—a truth that often must be wrested from deceit.

Wesley's life and practice remain relevant in the twenty-first century in large measure because of the biblical order of salvation he came to understand and the organization into which that pathway to Christian maturity grew. Wesley's way of discipleship became a model of spiritual formation. Welcome to a journey of engagement with beliefs and disciplines that have across the years been means of grace to change lives.

Looking for a Pathway

In the first decade of the twenty-first century one of the high-profile megachurches in the world, Willow Creek Community Church, asked themselves the question "How do you know if people are growing closer to Christ?" Another way of putting the question was, "Is our church really helping people become devoted followers of Christ, or are we just giving them a nice place to go to church?" They developed a research tool, the Reveal Spiritual Life Survey, which was subsequently used by over a quarter million people in a thousand churches, diverse in size, denomination, and geography. What they discovered sounds like the template of Wesleyan spiritual formation.

It became clear that people who participated in those surveys were looking for a pathway to follow, much like the Wesleyan understanding of how grace engages people from its prevenient beginnings (the before-you-know-it stage) to perfection (loving God and neighbor as the primary purpose of life). It also became clear that structures providing loving accountability (small groups) were crucial. Finding ways to get people on bridges intentionally built into the local community was also a key component of spiritual growth. For those familiar with Wesleyan piety, this is a description of Wesleyan spiritual DNA.[2]

Top 10 Methodist Beliefs is about the first element of this DNA, the scriptural pathway of spiritual formation as understood and communicated by John Wesley.

Most people do not jump to salute when doctrine is run up the flagpole. Doctrine is not sexy. If major television networks and cable channels look for programs that will get high ratings, they do not seek out programming featuring religious doctrine. In addition to such obstacles, Wesley himself would have been quick to agree that religious knowledge is no guarantee of discipleship.

Unless we are prepared to throw out the Bible, we must accept the necessity of doctrine or sound, reliable teaching.

But unless we are prepared to throw out the Bible, we must accept the necessity of doctrine or sound, reliable teaching. There are people who argue that "doctrine divides," but they are not people who have no doctrines. The idea that doctrine divides and therefore should be jettisoned is a doctrine.

All of us have interpretations of matters of faith. As one who sought above all to be a scriptural Christian, Wesley believed that such conclusions have both immediate and eternal results. Consequently, while he was smart enough to understand the pitfalls of doctrinal study, Wesley was also wise enough to know that sound doctrine is an inescapable and ultimately invaluable part of being a follower of Jesus Christ.

It is true that if you are hungry and someone gives you a bowl of soup it doesn't matter if or how they were baptized. But if you have been baptized, what you think that means may have a very direct influence on whether or not you take food to the hungry. Doctrinal issues can be controversial, confusing, and plain contrary. But they can also be a tool of the Spirit to bring life!

Scriptural Teaching: Can You Stand the Excitement?

Welcome to a challenging and potentially very stimulating world, the world of biblical doctrine. It is part of what the Apostle Paul had in mind when he spoke of "fear and trembling" as inherent to the Christian life (Phil 2:12). This is a battle. Describing such a struggle in his letter to the Ephesian church, the seasoned apostle used turbulent, almost violent images (Eph 4:14). Those new Christ-followers were being "tossed and blown around by every wind that comes from teaching with deceitful scheming and the tricks people play to deliberately mislead others."

To the young church in Corinth he wrote, "They destroy arguments, and every defense that is raised up to oppose the knowledge of God. They capture every thought to make it obedient to Christ" (2 Cor 10:4-5). This is hand-to-hand combat intended to do what all sound Christian doctrine does: clear the way for truth/the Truth to set us free. For any who want a more-than-forgiveness faith, such combat is not a luxury or an option. The purpose of scripture is not just to provide material for the communion ritual. Scripture, animated by the very breath of God, is a tool for battle: for teaching, for reproof, for correction, and for training in righteousness, that the person of God may be complete, equipped for every good work (2 Tim 3:16).

The Apostle Paul's final pastoral word to the Ephesian church is to prepare for this very real battle by putting on the whole armor of God (the centerpiece of which is the belt of truth) to defeat evil (the core of which is lies). Our lives in Christ are an unrelenting fight, a good fight (2 Tim 4:7), but still a fight. Such a fight calls for diligence to take hold of that for which Christ has taken hold of us (Phil 3:12).

When John Wesley went to battle, it was not to produce copies of himself. He wanted to help sinners engage grace and become more and more fully engaged with their Lord. Doctrines are signposts to such ends, not hitching posts. They point us beyond themselves to the Way, the Truth, and the Life whom we follow. Everyone lives according to signposts of some kind. As in any journey, Wesley was passionate about following the signposts set out in scripture in order to fully follow Jesus. What a great tradition!

Doctrines are signposts, not hitching posts. They point us beyond themselves to the Way, the Truth, and the Life whom we follow.

Christian Are Always in a Battle—a Battle for Abundant Living

Earlier in my ministry I served near the Kings Bay Naval Submarine base in southeast Georgia. It is the East Coast home to the Trident submarine fleet. The Trident fleet is equipped with approximately 50 percent of the thermonuclear weaponry of the United States military. As a pastor I was aware that some of the people I served were part of a destructive force that could end the world as we know it in a matter of minutes. The point of such power is to discourage similar attacks by enemies, but I lived with an awareness of the consequences of any failure to manage such power.

As a pastor I know, thankfully, most people do not live with such monumental possibilities. Even so, I am keenly aware, because I have observed it up close for decades, that all of us have power to build or to destroy our own lives. Fortunately Jesus did not say, "I have come so that you might not destroy your life" or "I have come so that you could develop major defenses against failure or destruction." He said, "I came so that they could have life—indeed, so that they could live to the fullest" (John 10:10). John Wesley labored to help people not only avoid self-destruction and be saved from the worst that might happen but to help people take seriously the holy, abundant potential God has made possible in Jesus Christ.

The discipline of Methodist societies was serious business. A good beginning, like a good takeoff, was only of value if the final landing was safe and secure. John Wesley literally lived in a kind of warfare, often attacked by mobs and, for a time, expelled from Anglican pulpits. Yet he continued to proclaim what he was convinced were the historic teachings of scripture. Theologian Kevin Vanhoozer has written that the task of theology "is to enable hearers and doers of the gospel to respond and to correspond to the prior Word and Act of God, and thus to be drawn into the action."[3] When in 1749 Charles Wesley penned the words to "Soldiers of Christ, Arise," he wedded an awareness of battle with a call to live in God's grace and "thus to be drawn into the action."[4]

I Once Was Looking but Then I Got Found, and Other Spiritual Bifocals

The Wesley brothers' lives would become living examples of the words penned by an anonymous poet who wrote:

I sought the Lord, and afterward I knew
He moved my soul to seek him, seeking me.
It was not I that found, O Savior true;
No, I was found of thee.[5]

Once "found," a fire burned in Wesley's heart to enable any and all, especially common people, to have unhindered access to the good news of Jesus Christ. In the first volume of his *Sermons for Several Occasions* (1746) he wrote, "I design plain truth for plain people." Plain truth meant essential biblical teaching, unvarnished by philosophical spin, refusing to tranquilize the message of the cross and the high calling. John Wesley was a keenly intelligent thinker with an encyclopedic knowledge of the Bible. Part of his efforts at speaking plainly included a willingness to state briefly what he believed to be the essence of the gospel. He identified the following three essentials of a Christ-following life:

- repentance
- faith
- holiness

Plain truth, however, did not imply sacrificing the paradoxes of a relationship with God as revealed in the breadth of scripture. Salvation as a gift of God meant work! Had such wardrobe witnesses existed in the eighteenth century, the front of the John Wesley class meeting T-shirt might have proclaimed in bold print:

We are saved by grace through faith!

The back might have said:

Wimps need not apply!

Twentieth-century English theologian G. K. Chesterton spoke of the paradoxical contradictions in the gospel as "furious opposites."[6] Seeking to understand Wesley's interpretation of basic doctrines does not require surrendering theological depth, texture, and nuance on the altar of simplicity. Wesley was adept at keeping more than one theological ball in the air at a time. This skill keeps his interpretation and application of the Christian faith interesting as well as dynamic and true to life and scripture.

Plain truth meant essential biblical teaching, unvarnished by philosophical spin. Plain truth, however, did not imply sacrificing the paradoxes of a relationship with God as revealed in the breadth of scripture.

Hopefully as you reflect on Wesley's thinking you will find it deeply satisfying to sense the integrity with which he seeks to be true to the written Word and to life. This is the rich birthright of United Methodism and others in the Wesleyan family.

Conjunctive Theology: Not an Either/Or, but a Both/And View of Truth

Developing an understanding *and* application of the scriptural message was always Wesley's goal. So it is necessary to come to terms with what may appear to be contradictory, furious opposites:

- The first shall be last.
- Find your life by losing it.
- Work out your salvation with fear and trembling, for it is God who works in you.
- Where sin abounds, there grace abounds much more.

At the heart of the gospel is the great paradox "He saved others, . . . but he can't save himself" (Mark 15:31). Doctrines possessing potentially conflicted concepts include:

- law *and* grace
- justification *and* sanctification
- faith *and* works
- instantaneousness *and* process
- divine initiative *and* human response
- the necessary nature of amazing grace *and* its limited freedom to control

Part of what has made Wesley's thinking enduring was his capacity to teach plainly without settling for partial understanding of the whole picture. In his sermon "The Law Established Through Faith," we can view an example in the bifocal, conjunctive (both/and rather than either/or) synthesis characteristic of Wesley with regard to faith and works.

> The truth lies between both. We are doubtless, "justified by faith." This is the corner-stone of the whole Christian building. "We are justified without works of the law" as any previous condition of justification. But they are an immediate fruit of that faith whereby we are justified. So that if good works do not follow our faith, even all inward and outward holiness, it is plain our faith is nothing worth; we are yet in our sins.[7]

Giving works such credence led to conflicts with those who saw salvation as God's solo action (mostly these were identified as Calvinists). Wesley refused to give in to one side of truth at the cost of a broader understanding of scripture and human experience, even if he sympathized with its importance. It is easier to be simplistic, yes, but far more satisfying and honest to wrestle with questions and conflicts until they yield a comprehensive view of truth.

This struggle to coordinate the relationships between truths brings to mind the seemingly contradictory approach in which some people wear

contact lenses called monovision. In order to correct both nearsighted-
ness and farsightedness, it is possible to wear a different prescription in
each eye. This solves both sight problems because of the brain's ability
to coordinate varying magnifications. The result is clear vision both up
close and distant. Wesley's theology allows for the need for such coordination between apparent opposites.

An example of "both/and" "conjunctive"
synthesis is seen in Wesley's concern
for the basic message of justification
by faith and the call to sanctification/
holiness.

An example of "both/and" "conjunctive" synthesis is seen in Wesley's
concern for the basic message of justification by faith and the call to
sanctification/holiness. Albert Outler, a major voice in Wesleyan studies
in the twentieth century, created an inventory of Wesley's sermon texts.
Outler learned that Wesley's first six favorite texts "were all variations on
the central evangelical message: *repent and accept God's grace in Christ!*
The most frequently used scripture text was Mark 1:15, 'Repent ye, and
believe the gospel.'"[8]
Obviously Wesley was willing to focus on part of salvation, understanding that the journey to a whole faith begins with initial steps.
However, he was deeply convinced that salvation as justification/pardon
alone was not scriptural salvation. Justification is initial sanctification
and should be the doorway into a life of maturing holy discipleship. In
1778, writing to a woman named Mary Bishop, he made this clear: "Let
but a pert, self-sufficient animal, that has neither sense nor grace, bawl
out something about Christ and His blood or justification by faith, and
his hearers cry out, 'What a fine gospel sermon!' Surely the Methodists

have not so learnt Christ. We know of no gospel without salvation from sin."[9]

British pastor Charles Simeon, whose ministry was maturing as Wesley's was concluding, expressed this dynamic in these words: "Truth is not in the middle, and not in one extreme, but in both extremes."[10] A twentieth-century voice, pastor, and author, A. W. Tozer affirmed this necessity of biblical interpretation:

> Truths that are compelled to stand alone never stand straight and are not likely to stand for long. Truth is one but truths are many. Scriptural truths are interlocking and interdependent. A truth is rarely valid in isolation. A statement may be true in its relation to other truths, but less than true when separated from them. Truth is like a bird. It cannot fly on one wing. Yet we are forever trying to take off with one wing flapping furiously and the other tucked neatly out of sight.[11]

Wesley scholar Paul Chilcote has written a study, *Recapturing the Wesleys' Vision*, which illustrates how fundamental it is to the Wesleys' grasp of authentic Christian faith and practice to maintain tension, balance, and coordination among biblical affirmations. In other words this is a "conjunctive," both/and synthesis of truth. He notes an example of simultaneous love of neighbor and self from *Plain Account of Genuine Christianity* and offers a comment:

> "By experience he knows that *social love* (if it mean the love of our neighbour) is absolutely, essentially different from *self-love*, even of the most allowable kind, just as different as the objects at which they point. And yet it is sure that, if they are under due regulations, each will give additional force to the other...." There can be no separation of self-love and neighbor-love in the life of the Christian. Genuine love of self that is rooted in God's affirmation—God's prior love—must find expression in love of others. The two must be held together.[12]

Other possible conflicting spiritual poles that Wesley saw as complementary and conjunctive include:

- personal piety and compassionate outreach
- a personal relationship with God and corporate interaction with other believers
- faith in the heart and faith in the head
- worship in the word and worship at the sacramental table
- freedom in the spirit and order/discipline
- human freedom and God's sovereignty

Wesley scholar Richard Heitzenrater sees this pattern of juggling opposites as an element woven throughout Wesley's life.

> Wesley was an educated upper-class Oxford don who spent most of his life working among the poor and disadvantaged. This paradoxical lifestyle left its mark on the character of many of his activities. He was a champion of the poor, yet a defender of the political establishment that had caused many of their problems. He was a master of expression in several languages, yet strove to express "plain truth for plain people." In his outlook and activities, he attempted to unite, in his brother Charles's words, "the pair so long disjoined, knowledge and vital piety." He combined in his ministry the preaching of the revivalist and the concerns of the social worker. His religious perspective was at the same time evangelical and sacramental. If we fail to keep in mind this tendency to hold seeming opposites together in unity (though not without some internal tension), we will miss one of the significant keys to understanding his life and thought.[13]

In his remarkable *Lectures on Preaching* (1877), nineteenth-century American clergyman Phillips Brooks defined preaching as "truth through personality."[14] John Wesley's pursuit of the truth that sets us free (John 8:32-36) was shepherded by a personality that relentlessly sought to live out "the entire plan of God" (Acts 20:27). Frankly, there are times when it appears if Wesley is talking out of both sides of his theological mouth. That is why it is always important to note the context and timing of his statements. His unwillingness to settle for simplistic scriptural interpretation would sometimes lead him to emphasize one side of both/and truths—God's sovereignty or human response—for example, in order to avoid error or exaggeration on the other side.

Wesley understood doctrine as a means to an end and not the end of Christian discipleship. His deep concern was to understand and defend right doctrine in order to release the truth it conveyed. He wrestled with doctrine so as to move beyond it to the transforming intention of the Spirit who inspired it. The bridges of his "both/and" conjunctive theology are the pathways that his relentless search discovered were not only true but life-giving. For example, to emphasize either faith or works would have been easier but far less satisfying than to work through to a clear understanding that they do not conflict but complement each other. Do not see this as an academic exercise. It is the necessary work of fleshing out the implications of your salvation.

> *Wesley understood doctrine as a means to an end and not the end of Christian discipleship. He wrestled with doctrine so as to move beyond it to the transforming intention of the Spirit who inspired it.*

Phillips Brooks mirrors Wesley's priority of transformation over information when he says, "Much of our preaching is like delivering lectures upon medicine to sick people... to give the medicine, not to deliver the lecture, is the preacher's duty."[15] Wesley was profoundly committed to the vital necessity of both prescribing (doctrine) and administering (ministry) the correct medicine. This meant wide-ranging reading and study. G. K. Chesterton once observed that the object of opening the mind was similar to opening the mouth: to close it on something firm.[16] Along with scripture and authoritative traditional writings, Wesley sampled the intellectual buffet of his day and came to a sure conclusion as to the source of authoritative prescriptions for the human predicament. The chapters ahead will flesh out Wesley's conjunctive balance between orthodoxy (right knowing) and orthopraxy (right doing).

Questions for Discussion

1. The term *doctrine* comes from the word for "teaching." What does doctrine mean to you?

2. Why would doctrine matter to followers of Jesus Christ?

3. Do you see yourself as in a battle to believe and live as Jesus would have you believe and live? Describe that battle.

4. If we are saved by God's gift of grace received by faith, why might it be said, "Wimps need not apply!"?

5. What did Wesley mean when he spoke of faith and works in a believer's life, "the truth lies between both"?

6. How does wrestling with "both/and" issues help us to be more fully engaged followers of Jesus Christ?

B e l i e f # 1

Scripture Is Our Primary Source

Who or what do you obey? What will guide the way you live today?

It's a huge question. For the Wesleys the answer, while not simple, was clear. The Bible was their guide. The Methodists were eventually called "Bible bigots." As a student at Oxford, Charles Wesley discovered, as had John three years earlier, that "a man stands a very fair chance of being laughed out of his religion at his first setting out."[1] That did not deter their commitment to the authority of scripture. The question with which the Bible presented them as they understood it was not, "How can I believe this?" The question was, "What is God saying and how can I obey it?" As we shall see, their faith in the Bible was not wooden and rigid in a fundamentalist sense. Neither was it subject to their whims or the correctness of the day. They earnestly sought to trust and obey God's Word, and while that made them fruitful, it also brought derision and rejection as well as controversy.

Just saying, "I believe in the Bible" does not end the battle as to the nature of its authority. As always, we see in Wesley's example a willingness to move beyond a simplistic "God said it; I believe it; that's good enough for me" response to scripture. But to do that opens the door to broad possibilities of interpretation. Wesley accepted this as the price for honest faith. It is not a matter for the faint of heart.

Wesley instinctively understood that orthodoxy is no guarantee of spiritual vitality. His desire was to unleash…God's Word and allow it maximum freedom to move beyond the letter to the transformative spirit of truth.

Church of England theologians (Bishop Joseph Butler chief among them), in the face of intellectual challenges from persons such as John Locke and Sir Isaac Newton, defended biblical authority. So did John Wesley. The scriptures were, for Wesley, "the fountain of heavenly wisdom, which they who are able to taste prefer to all writings of men, however wise or learned or holy."[2] His view of the supremacy of scripture would never waver throughout his long journey. While this was of utmost importance to Wesley, he instinctively understood that orthodoxy is no guarantee of spiritual vitality. His desire was to unleash what he firmly believed to be God's Word and allow it maximum freedom to move beyond the letter to the transformative spirit of truth. For Wesley this was not an academic exercise. It was, as it remains today, a battle for abundant life.

Wesley characteristically affirms the uniqueness and authority of scripture in the *Preface to Sermons on Several Occasions*: "I want to know one thing, the way to heaven—how to land safe on that happy shore.…He hath written it down in a book. O give me that book! At any price give me the book of God! I have it. Here is knowledge enough for me. Let me be *homo unius libri* (a man of one book)."[3]

In the same way that he embraced the derisive identification "Methodist" as a badge of honor, Wesley gladly endured the sneering epithets "Bible bigot" and "Bible moth." He wrote in *A Short History of Methodism* (1765) that in February 1738, the fledgling Methodists "resolved to be Bible-Christians at all events; and, what ever they were, to preach with all their might plain, old, Bible Christianity."[4] A year later he wrote in a letter to Oxford friend James Hervey, "I allow no other rule, whether of faith or practice, than the holy Scriptures."[5] Fifty years later he would write in other correspondence, "be not wise above what is written. Enjoin nothing that the Bible does not clearly enjoin. Forbid nothing that it clearly does not forbid."[6] The normative authority of the Bible in Wesley's theological method is beyond debate.

The Bible: Its Best Defense Is to Turn It Loose

British Reformed Baptist preacher Charles Spurgeon, in the century following Wesley, famously said that scripture is like a lion, it does not need defense. Rather it needs to be turned loose.[7] Wesley, who did not apply his best powers of logic to defending the Bible, would have liked that image. Nonetheless, he dutifully penned a brief tract entitled "A Clear and Concise Demonstration of the Divine Inspiration of Holy Scripture."[8] At best, his defense of scripture falls under the general principle that New Testament scholar Joel Green observed regarding such efforts: "Arguments in favor of the special status of the Scriptures tend to be convincing only to those who are already inclined to grant them this status."[9] Wesley was far more burdened to turn scripture loose than to academically defend it, believing it would prove itself to others as it had to him.

Wesley was far more burdened to turn scripture loose than to academically defend it, believing it would prove itself to others as it had to him.

In the preface to Wesley's *Explanatory Notes Upon the New Testament*, we find this expanded affirmation of faith in scripture:

3

Concerning the Scriptures in general, it may be observed, the word of the living God, which directed the first patriarchs also, was, in the time of Moses, committed to writing. To this were added, in several succeeding generations, the inspired writings of the other prophets. Afterwards, what the Son of God preached, and the Holy Ghost spake by the apostles, the apostles and evangelists wrote. This is what we now style the Holy Scripture: this is that "word of God which remaineth for ever"; of which, though "heaven and earth pass away, one jot or tittle shall not pass away." The Scripture, therefore, of the Old and New Testament is a most solid and precious system of divine truth. Every part thereof is worthy of God; and all together are one entire body, wherein is no defect, no excess.[10]

Wesley's commentary in his *Notes* on 2 Timothy 3:16 declares:

All scripture is inspired by God – The Spirit of God not only inspired those who wrote it, but continually inspires, supernaturally assists, those that read it with earnest prayer. Hence *it is* so *profitable for doctrine*, for instruction of the ignorant, *for* the *reproof* or conviction of them that are in error or sin, *for* the *correction* or amendment of whatever is amiss, and for instructing or training up children of God *in* all *righteousness*.[11]

Wesley's unrestrained dedication to the uniqueness and supremacy of the Bible was directly tied to his unshakable focus on leading others to justification (pardon), sanctification (growing love of God and neighbor/the mind of Christ), and glorification (ultimately the way to heaven). Apart from the Bible, is evangelism and making disciples possible? Wesley knew that it was not.

Wesley: A Man of One Totally Unique Book

Imagine a compulsively rational person, a lover of logic whose mother said he would not "attend to the necessities of nature"[12] (go to the bathroom) without a reason; now picture this man crying out from the depths of his soul, "O Give me that book! At any price give me that book! I have it. Here is enough knowledge for me."[13]

Wesley was a man of letters, an Oxford don, a translator and publisher of poetry, a man who wrote hundreds of books, a spiritual director of thousands who created a Christian library for their edification, who edited *Pilgrim's Progress* for the masses, whose literary production of letters, sermons, and responses to theological controversies now comprise multiplied numbers of volumes—this person repeatedly declares, "Let me be a man of one book." Wesley embraced the declaration that "all scripture is inspired by God" and thus reflects an unrivaled divine authority. The written word then plays a categorically unique role in the birthing and formation of Christian disciples. As the decades of the revival went by, he witnessed the power of the written word to facilitate living engagement with the living Word, the risen Jesus.

A startling example of the power of the Bible to provide such compelling, divine testimony can be witnessed in the life of Princeton Seminary professor of philosophy Emile Cailliet. Cailliet was born and intellectually bred to embrace a purely naturalistic view of life. In his theological autobiography, *Journey Into Light*, he remembers an upbringing lacking even "a hint that God may intervene to guide anyone or ordain anything to some providential end He had in view."[14]

In the muddy and bloody trenches of World War I, not as an academic exercise but as a brutally urgent preoccupation, Cailliet questioned the meaning of life based on presuppositions that categorically rejected supernatural intrusion into human experience. The words of Scottish poet James Thomson framed the essential pessimism of his naturalistic outlook:

> every struggle brings defeat
> Because Fate holds no prize to crown success;
> That all the oracles are dumb to cheat
> Because they have no secret to express,
> That none can pierce the vast black veil uncertain

Because there is no light beyond the curtain;
That all is vanity and nothingness. (*Stanza xxi*)[15]

One night Cailliet was hit by a bullet and would spend the next nine months recovering in an American hospital. During his recovery, he married a Scotch-Irish girl he had met prior to the war. Her upbringing could hardly have differed more from his. As a child, her parents had seen to it that she attended both the low Church of England and Presbyterian Sunday Schools. However, Calliet made it clear to her that religion would be taboo in their home.

When he later resumed his academic studies, Cailliet experienced a new longing for substance. He wrote, "During long night watches in the foxholes I had in a strange way been longing—I must say it, however queer it may sound—for a book that would understand me. But I knew of no such book."[16] So, fertile thinker that Cailliet was, he secretly began an effort to create such a book. Reading for various academic courses, he would file away passages that spoke "to his condition." A leather-bound book in which such carefully noted insights were filed was his constant companion.

The day finally arrived when it seemed "the book that would understand me" was complete. Sitting beneath a shade tree, he commenced contemplation of the anthology. To his great disappointment, no epiphany emerged. The various passages only reminded him of their origins and his efforts in collecting them. "Then I knew," he concluded, "that the whole undertaking would not work, simply because it was of my own making. It carried no strength of persuasion."[17]

At that very moment his wife, who knew nothing of this project, appeared at the gate of their garden. Anticipating a negative, if not hostile reaction, she nonetheless related the events of her afternoon. In the sunny heat she had taken their baby for a stroll in the baby carriage. The main boulevard was very crowded, so she took a bumpy cobblestone side street, eventually stopping on a grassy spot to rest.

The patch of grass led to a stone staircase that she navigated with the baby carriage, almost without thinking. At the top was an open door through which could be seen a long room. Curious, she entered. At the far end of the room was a white-haired man. Seeing a carving of a cross it dawned on her that this was a Huguenot church. Built in the day when persecution was an ever-present threat, it was off the beaten path.

Tentatively approaching the venerable-looking man, she learned that he was a pastor. Without forethought she spontaneously asked, "Have you a Bible in French?" Smiling, he handed her a copy, which she eagerly took with a mixture of joy and guilt. Now, standing before her unbelieving husband, she hesitated to try and give an account of how it all seemed to happen without logical explanation. But Calliet was no longer listening to her story.

"A Bible, you say? Where is it? Show me. I have never seen one before!"[18]

He literally grabbed the book out of her hand and rushed to his study. The Bible opened "by chance" to the Beatitudes. He read and read and read, feeling an indescribable warmth within. Awe and wonder filled his mind. "And suddenly the realization dawned upon me: This *was* the Book that would understand me!" He continued reading into the night, mostly from the Gospels. "And lo and behold, as I looked through them, the One of whom they spoke, the One who spoke and acted in them, became alive to me."

> A decisive insight flashed through my whole being the following morning as I probed the opening chapters of the gospel according to John. The very clue to the secret of human life was disclosed right there, not stated in the foreboding language of philosophy, but in the common, everyday language of human circumstances. And far from moving on their own accord, these circumstances seemed to yield themselves without striving obedient unto One who inexorably stood out from the gospel narrative—indeed a Person of far more than human nature and stature.[19]

7

Would it not be appropriate to imagine this person of letters declaring, "Let me be a man of one book!" One book is in a class of its own, "the oracles of God" Wesley would call it, harkening back to 1 Peter 4.

Scripture: Normative but Not Alone

If you are a person who values insights from cultures both present and past, you will appreciate that John Wesley was also a man of many other books, a man who "plundered the Egyptians." This term was first used by Origen, one of the most influential writers in the early centuries of the Christian movement. The idea comes from Exodus 12:18-36 where the Israelites, as they departed from Egypt, took along with them "gifts" from their former masters. Albert Outler in *Theology in the Wesleyan Spirit* explains the term: Plundering the Egyptians "is a *metaphor* pointing to the freedom that Christians have (by divine allowance) to explore, appraise, and appropriate all the insights and resources of any and all secular culture."[20] St. Augustine would later borrow this metaphor to justify his own reappraisal of classical culture. Wesley likewise plundered the Egyptians.

To the great majority of those hearing Wesley preach, his liberal arts education was a kind of intellectual karate, bolstering but not dominating. He was serious about plain truth for plain people. Early Wesley historian John Telford records a story Wesley told concerning a fledgling attempt at preaching, which left the congregation open-mouthed. A second attempt left their mouths half open. He then read the sermon to an intelligent servant named Betty. Every time she said, "Stop," he would make a revision until it was understandable to her.[21] While comfortable with a larger intellectual world, Wesley was not a slave to the pride of knowledge that so easily puffs up (1 Cor 8:1). His broad education was made to serve the kingdom of God rather than his ego.

Behind the preaching of this folk theologian was a staggering capacity to entertain a wide range of intellectual and cultural interests. His record of materials read includes more than fourteen hundred different authors. Though generally written for mass consumption, his sermons were sprinkled with quotations from men of letters such as Horace (who coined the term *carpe diem*), Virgil, Ovid, and Cicero. Five paragraphs after defining himself as a man of one book, Wesley quotes from Homer's *Iliad* in the Greek language.[22] Plato, Aristotle, and Augustine were familiar sources. He quoted freely from Shakespeare and Milton. Dr. Samuel Johnson, a towering figure in British literary history, was a friend, though Wesley's refusal to sit and converse for extended periods of conversation was known to aggravate Johnson greatly.

In addition to literature, Wesley read all of the "modern science" at his disposal, being conversant, for example, in the work of Isaac Newton. And while he generally denounced the theater of his day, his writings reveal what Outler termed an "extensive acquaintance" with English drama. An avid student of languages, Wesley wrote grammars in seven of the eight languages he knew: Hebrew, Greek, Latin, French, German, Dutch, Spanish, and Italian. He compiled a *Christian Library* of fifty volumes of material he abridged for Wesleyan purposes. Other "compendia" included *A Survey of the Wisdom of God in Creation, History of England,* and *Ecclesiastical History.* The *Arminian Magazine* appeared in 1778 as a tool to combat similar publications that promoted Calvinism; it also served as a kind of religious *Reader's Digest.* Wesley's *Journal* reflected a life that British historian Henry Rack, not a Wesley apologist, affirmed as a "superior" mirror of the eighteenth century owing to the fact that "Wesley had the advantage of moving easily and without affectation between the very different worlds of the mob, the respectable artisan and tradesman, and the educated middling classes."[23]

There was only one "middle C" in Wesley's life and it was scripture. If a different note came from even the loftiest source, it must conform to that one middle C.

Wesley wrote *Notes* on the Old and New Testaments, volumes of correspondence, sermons, textbooks for children, as well as books on primitive medicine and electricity. With the scriptures as his compass, he traveled the world of ideas in his day and mined them for any witness they could make to the Lord of all. In so doing, he understood that scripture had to be interpreted and that would best be done with appropriate, albeit limited, tools.

Wesley's dedication to the authority of scripture could imply that his life was intellectually and theologically circumscribed. Obviously that was not the case. Still, there was only one middle C in his life and it was scripture. If a different note came from even the loftiest source, it must conform to that one middle C, not vice versa. With that in place he could wisely use the other notes the world makes available to compose the symphonies of doctrine that were vitally important to the making of disciples. Wesley happily wrestled with the reality that even an authoritative Bible required interpretation. With methodical qualifications, he would embrace the tools of interpretation that give integrity to interpreting "the message of truth correctly" (2 Tim 2:15).

Questions for Discussion

1. Have you ever been made fun of because of your faith? Describe.

2. What did Wesley mean by saying he wanted to be "a man of one book"?

3. Has the Bible "proven itself" in your life? If so, how?

4. Why was Cailliet unsatisfied with the book he had created? What did he learn from that?

5. Augustine is quoted as having said, "If you believe what you like in the gospel and reject what you don't like, it's not the gospel you believe but yourself." What do you think of that idea and how might it apply to scripture?

6. How has your trust of the Bible been challenged? How have you responded to that?

7. Earlier in the chapter Wesley's comments on 2 Timothy 3:16 are quoted. What was the Apostle Paul saying about the authority of scripture?

Belief #2

Reason, Tradition, and Experience Help Us Understand Scripture

Wouldn't it be great if we just opened the Bible, pushed a button, and heard the voice of God explain the meaning of each passage as it is read? Holden Caulfield in *The Catcher in the Rye* lamented, "What really knocks me out about a book that, when you're all done reading it, you wish the author that wrote it was a terrific friend of yours and you could call him up on the phone whenever you felt like it. That doesn't happen much, though."[1] Wouldn't it be great to have that kind of access to God who inspired the Bible's pages? Well, as Holden observed, that doesn't happen much, not literally. Why not?

Our heavenly Father, the ultimate wise parent, knows that unless children learn to take responsibility for themselves, there will be no maturity. We are designed to be fully engaged in the challenge of life, including the life of faith. Jesus's call was and is a call to unabashed participation: "Repent!" "Seek first the kingdom of God and his righteousness!" "Abide in me!" "Take my yoke upon you!" "Love your neighbor!" "Go therefore and make disciples of all nations!" It is not surprising that Wesley's message and methods included active and disciplined human

13

participation with tools he found to be necessary in understanding and applying scripture.

In the later part of the twentieth century the term *Wesleyan quadrilateral* was coined as a way of identifying the means and methods routinely used by Wesley to understand God's will and ways. **Scripture**, as affirmed in the previous chapter, is the unique, authoritative source of truth, the foundation of the four elements. Since there isn't a button we can push to get a direct interpretation of scripture from God, the common tools needed to discern the message of scripture included: **reason**, **tradition**, and **experience**. Admittedly, considering the quadrilateral can feel academic. But for Wesley a proper use of these elements was not a luxury for academics but the very stuff of rightly dividing the word of truth (2 Tim 2:15) in order to walk as Jesus walked.

The term Wesleyan quadrilateral *was coined as a way of identifying the means and methods routinely used by Wesley to understand God's will and ways.*

Reason: A Reasonable, Though Incomplete, Place to Begin

John Wesley taught logic at Oxford and would well understand the nature of reason. In a sermon entitled "The Case of Reason Impartially Considered" (#70), he called for balance in appreciating but not overvaluing reason. Some of his peers, influenced by Enlightenment thinking, thought that reason could replace divine revelation. Reason, they declared, was "the all sufficient director of all the children of men."[2] Wesley disagreed. The better way, he concluded, is a middle road that values reason as a necessary tool in the processing of information, but remains "utterly incapable of giving either faith, hope or love." With regard to such qualities, he wrote, "Expect these from a higher source, even the Father of the spirits of all flesh."[3]

Clearly, reason is necessary. Wesley firmly said that "to renounce reason is to renounce religion…and…all irrational religion is false religion."[4] Reason allows us to communicate by establishing logical guidelines that are shared across communities and cultures. Of course, we also know that emotions often masquerade as reason and personal interests can "spin" reason to a desired outcome. How, then, does it rise to a place of serious usefulness? For Wesley, the explanation was found in the proactive grace of God in conjunction with scripture (reasonably studied with trusted methods). This grace, at first unrecognized as it works in a human life, enables the possibility of faith. As faith opens the door to new life in Christ (Eph 2:8-9), among the results are "spiritual senses." He writes,

> But the moment the Spirit of the Almighty strikes the heart of him that was till then without God in the world, it breaks the hardness of his heart, and creates all things new.…The Sun of Righteousness appears, and shines upon his soul, showing him the light of the glory of God in the face of Jesus Christ.…By the same gracious stroke he that before had ears but heard not is now made capable of *hearing*.…At the same time he receives other spiritual senses, capable of discerning spiritual good and evil.[5]

Even though reason could be thus enlightened, reason nonetheless was not *normative*. Scripture was always the standard setting source for Christian thinking. For Wesley the active grace of God in conjunction with scripture was the key to the proper employment of reason. All caveats aside, Wesley was, as usual, reasonable in supporting reason as necessary to all rational discourse, including discourse in religion.

For Wesley the active grace of God in conjunction with scripture was the key to the proper employment of reason.

15

In Luke 20, Jesus's parable of the tenants allegorically describes the reaction of Jewish leaders to Jesus, comparing it to tenant farmers who won't respect the owner's rights. As the story goes, when the owner decides to send his son in the hope of a positive response, we're told that the tenants *reasoned* together and decided to kill the owner's son (KJV). The story is a cautionary tale about the danger of trusting human reason, even when it is the result of conferencing!

Tradition: For Wesley a Valuable but Limited Aid

When was the last time you read something written by Ignatius, Tertullian, Origen, or Ephrem Syrus? They are not well known to laypersons today, but were carefully studied by Wesley along with other Christian writers of the first three centuries. For Wesley tradition was not limited to, but was most valued from the early centuries, the religion of the *primitive church* or *Christian antiquity* as he called it (through the early fourth century). Serious respect for the "fathers" of the post–New Testament church was instilled in him by his father. In a seventy-nine-page letter written to the Reverend Dr. Conyers Middleton in 1749, Wesley endorses the writings of this early Christian period: "The esteeming the writings of the first three centuries, not equally with, but next to, the Scriptures, never carried any man yet into dangerous errors, nor probably ever will."[6]

Dr. Tom Oden, whose interest in these early writings led him to become general editor of the twenty-six-volume *Ancient Christian Commentary on Scripture*, cites the father of Methodism, saying, "Wesley was quick to concede that the ancient Christian writers made many occasional 'mistakes, many weak suppositions, and many ill-drawn conclusions.' Nonetheless [Wesley continued], 'I exceedingly reverence them as well as their writings... because they describe true, genuine Christianity.' "[7] Also part of this early witness to the faith was the ancient creeds—Nicene, Athanasian, and Apostles'.

Believing they reflected the teachings of the earliest writings, Anglican standard works such as the *Book of Common Prayer* and the *Homilies* were likewise considered authoritative. Another highly valued Anglican resource was Bishop John Pearson's commentary on the Apostles' Creed, for 250 years a standard text for Anglican theological students. This text contained 2,000 biblical notations and references to 440 ancient authors. Bishop Pearson took the view that "in Christianity there can be no important truth which is not ancient; and whatsoever is truly new, is certainly false."[8] Needless to say, Bishop Pearson's highly traditional commentary has fallen out of favor in theological training settings today.

Wesley's identification of tradition appropriate for the formation of theology appears very provincial two hundred plus years later.

Wesleyan church historian Ted Campbell captures Wesley's relationship to the ancient Christian traditions:

Wesley appealed to Christian antiquity, for example, as a model for personal attitudes and corporate institutions in the Evangelical Revival....He claimed ancient Christian precedents for the societies (the ancient catechetical process), love feasts (the ancient *agape* meal), and watchnights (the ancient vigils). He called upon ancient Christian teachings to support what he considered to be the Methodists' distinctive teachings about the nature of faith as spiritual experience, and the elements of the "way of salvation" that followed from thisAncient Christianity as a whole was portrayed as a model of belief and behavior set explicitly against the models for belief and behavior that eighteenth-century Christians had inherited (that is to say, their culture).[9]

If you are thinking, *This is a narrow view of tradition*, you are correct. Tradition is usually thought of as those beliefs and practices that have arisen from beyond the Bible and come to have authority within a culture. Many worship practices, such as how often communion is received and who is allowed to serve and receive it, are traditions. Wesley's identification of tradition appropriate for the formation of theology appears very provincial two hundred plus years later. We could not expect Wesley to imagine the expansion and diversity of the Christian movement in the centuries following his death.

Tradition: Growing Diversity

One of my wife's college roommates met Jesus through Methodist influences. That led to enrollment in an evangelical Wesleyan holiness college. She then did graduate work at an interdenominational Bible college. This was followed by a time of missionary service in a Central American country. She met and married a man who eventually attended a conservative Reformed seminary. From there they went on to serve in several very conservative Reformed congregations. The dominance of law masquerading as Christian tradition they experienced in those churches was so painful her husband left the pastoral ministry and found secular employment. Searching for a church experience more closely tied to the roots of Christianity, they eventually joined an Orthodox congregation.

This journey illustrates the variety of Christian traditions in which a contemporary life can be engaged. Part of what makes this story relevant is that the steadily building impetus behind it was strikingly sympathetic to the heart of Wesley. In the midst of personal struggle, this couple became motivated by a deep desire to return to an authentically New Testament faith, the faith of the *primitive* church. Church traditions had become obstacles to grace rather than means of grace, in their thinking.

Jesus had some harsh words for religious traditions: "You ignore God's commandment while holding on to rules created by humans and handed down to you.... Clearly, you are experts at rejecting God's commandment in order to establish these rules" (Mark 7:8-9). Isn't this a classic complaint of the prophets? Wasn't this the essential complaint of Martin Luther and other reformers?

First John 4:1, which Wesley knew very well, directs followers of Jesus to "test the spirits to see if they are from God." So it is with tradition. Clearly, authoritative *tradition*, in the sense in which it is included in the quadrilateral, has to have more behind it than, "We've always done it that way."

Experience: An Easily Misused Tool Wesley Would Not Lay Aside

John and Charles Wesley understood the Christian faith as more than ideas or theological propositions. Hence, in addition to reason and tradition as tools for theological formation, they included Christian experience as part of a holistic approach to following Jesus.

Of the four components of the quadrilateral, experience was the most troublesome. As controversial as affirming the place of experience in Christian living was, Wesley believed that the gospel had the power to enable all who believe to personally, subjectively, experience newness of life. He wrote concerning a friend, "The theory of religion he certainly has. May God give him the living experience of it."[10] For Wesley this was the meaning of "experience," the inner encounter with the Holy Spirit that confirmed what was revealed in scripture. Experience did not include every experience a person had ever had, as many today employ the term.

Wesley believed that the gospel had the power to enable all who believe to personally, subjectively, experience newness of life.

Nonetheless Wesley never relented from affirming and proclaiming the life-altering power of true religious experience. In the latter part of his life (1786) Wesley penned "Thoughts on Methodism," which included this straightforward declaration: "I am not afraid that the people called Methodists should ever cease to exist, either in Europe or America. But I am afraid, lest they should only exist as a dead sect, having the form of religion without the power. And this undoubtedly will be the case, unless they hold both the doctrine, spirit and discipline with which they first set out."[11]

John Wesley respected Christian experience as an empowering and crucial partner among these elements we now identify as the quadrilateral. Not everyone was as affirming of the value of experiential Christianity.

In eighteenth-century Great Britain, the popular name for religious extremists was *enthusiasts*. These were people who allowed experience—fully subjective understandings—to determine and dominate their beliefs and practices. Wesley, while affirming a rightful place for religious experience, adamantly refused to be tarred with the enthusiast brush. He repeatedly declared that his preaching was "plain old Bible Christianity." Methodism, he argued in spite of accusations of enthusiasm, was actually in the mainstream of scriptural tradition and he called the church to join them in seeking to live out the apostolic faith.

Why Did Accusations of Enthusiasm Persist?

Enthusiasm was associated with the practice of valuing personal experience over all other sources of authority. In his sermon "The Nature of Enthusiasm," Wesley offers a critique of this attitude, going so far as to call it "a religious madness arising from some falsely imagined influence or inspiration of God; at least from imputing something to God which ought not to be imputed to him, or expecting something from God which ought not to be expected from him."[12] Would this have described Wesley and those who followed him?

If you were an eighteenth-century Anglican, you could reasonably have put Wesley into the category of enthusiast. Why? Because he clearly, consistently, and aggressively declared the importance of what his contemporaries called *perceptible* inspiration.

Early in the revival (mid-1740s), Wesley exchanged a series of letters with the anonymous correspondent "John Smith." As their debate evolved, Wesley strongly affirmed his position on the subject of such subjective experience: "[We affirm] that inspiration of God's Holy Spirit whereby he fills us with righteousness, peace, and joy, with love to him and to all [people]. And we believe it cannot be, in the nature of things, that a [person] should be filled with this peace and joy and love...without perceiving it.... This is...the main doctrine of the Methodists."[13]

Wesley's best-known words, "My heart was strangely warmed," are reflective of the important place that perceptible inspiration has in Wesleyan piety. As is always the case when Wesley stubbornly clings to easily misunderstood or controversial teachings (such as Christian perfection), he does so because he is convinced they are biblical. Writing of the Holy Spirit's ordinary influences: love, joy, peace, long-suffering, gentleness, and meekness, he says, "Whoever has these, *inwardly feels* them. And if he understands his Bible, he discerns from whence they come."[14]

Assurance: The Common but Not Exactly Necessary Privilege of Believers

In terms of doctrine, it was his teaching on the experience of an assurance of pardon that led even Wesley himself to wrestle with the place and necessity of inward impressions in the Christian life. As in the above letter to "John Smith," John and Charles Wesley early on proclaimed that not only was assurance, as they often put it, "the common privilege of believers," but it was a necessary sign of true salvation. The minutes of the 1744 annual conference affirm this.[15] In a letter written to Charles Wesley three years later, he reasonably modifies this position by observing, "For how can a sense of our *having received* pardon be the condition of our receiving it?"[16]

Four decades later we read this report of the refining of Wesley's understanding of the relationship of assurance to saving faith:

> Nearly fifty years ago, when the Preachers, commonly called Methodists, began to preach that grand scriptural doctrine, salvation by faith, they were not sufficiently apprised of the difference between a servant and a child of God. They did not clearly understand, that even one "who feareth God and worketh righteousness, is accepted of him." In consequence of this, they were apt to make sad the hearts of those whom God had not made sad. For they frequently asked those who feared God, "Do you know that your sins are forgiven?" And upon their answering "No," immediately replied, "Then you are a child of the devil." No, that does not follow. It might be said, (and it is all that can be said with propriety.) "Hitherto you are only a servant, you are not a *child* of God. You have already great reason to praise God that he has called you to his honorable service. Fear not. Continue crying to unto him, 'And you shall see greater things than these.'"[17]

Perceptible inspiration from the Holy Spirit, which Wesley never stopped affirming, was understood as a desirable experience that can motivate and encourage. Perceptible inspiration was not, however, a final proof or basis for belief. As Wesley scholar Randy Maddox put it, Wesley viewed experience as having the power to *confirm* Christian claims, but he "specifically rejected the suggestion that he encouraged his followers to *derive* doctrine from such inner 'feelings.'"[18] Insofar as experience confirmed scripture it was embraced gladly.

> *Perceptible inspiration from the Holy Spirit was understood as a desirable experience that can motivate and encourage. Insofar as experience confirmed scripture it was embraced gladly.*

Perceptible inspiration was a victim of eighteenth-century political correctness. Wesley lived in the continuing wake of the English Commonwealth under Oliver Cromwell. That mid-seventeenth-century decade of conservative theocracy had left a bitter taste in the English mouth. Anything that smacked of religious zeal was greeted with suspicion if not hostility.

Even so, Wesley held firmly to the *reason*ableness of the impact of *scripturally* grounded *experience* as affirmed through *tradition* in Article XVII of the Thirty-nine Articles of the Church of England. This article of Anglican faith teaches that "godly persons feel in themselves the working of the Spirit of Christ, mortifying the works of the flesh . . . and drawing up their mind to high and heavenly things."[19]

As a pastor of forty-plus years I have witnessed the damage that unbridled enthusiasm can do. One scholar notes that experience "has contributed materially to that form of pluralism, verging on anarchy, which we now see across the Western world."[20] Many have seen congregations split apart when some members decide that their spiritual experiences are necessary for others in order to be "real" Christians. Frankly, there is no simple cure for this possibility. Such dangers partially explain why John and Charles were compulsively diligent and often apparently controlling in guiding the Methodist societies.

For John Wesley the high price of intense pastoral/spiritual care in the face of a movement marked by inner experiences of God's Spirit was a price he gladly paid in order to support a living faith, plain old Bible Christianity.

The Quadrilateral: Handle with Care

This look at Wesley's views of the four quadrilateral components opens windows of understanding into his thinking about scripture as the normative source of doctrine. At the same time it illustrates his realism in understanding that regardless of how high a view of scripture one might have, scripture must still be interpreted. The elements of the quadrilateral are not a formula that automatically produces agreement about valid doctrine or practice. Neither are they, as N. T. Wright put it, like different bookshelves, each of which can be ransacked for answers to key questions.[21] I recall hearing Wesley scholar William Abraham use a football analogy in describing how the quadrilateral can be abused. The idea was if scripture did not produce a desired result, then a lateral was made in order to justify a theological view, and on down the line. In his book *Waking from Doctrinal Amnesia* he observes the tendency in the formation of theology to use whichever component of the quadrilateral suits one's biases.

> The quadrilateral, even in its most carefully stated form, does not show how we are to resolve potential conflicts between the various sources. It is naive to think that, in a conflict between, say, scripture and reason, scripture will be allowed to carry the day.... The history of modern theology shows all too clearly that reason and experience will win every time over against scripture and tradition.[22]

Anglican scholar N. T. Wright echoes Abraham's observations:

> For Wesley himself, scripture remained the primary authority; the "experience" upon which he insisted was the living experience of God's love and the power of the Holy Spirit, through which what the Bible said was proved true in the life of the believer. It is quite an illegitimate use of all this to see "experience" as a separate source

of authority to be played off against scripture itself, though this move is now frequent, almost routine in many theological circles ("Scripture says...tradition says...reason says...but experience says...and so that's what we go with.")[23]

Wesley's best antidote was to stay as close to scripture as possible and participate in holy conferencing through the community's use of reason, tradition, and experience to interpret scripture. Following the account of the empty tomb in the final chapter of Luke's Gospel, there is a record of two disciples who encountered the risen Jesus while they "conversed and reasoned" (Luke 24:15 NKJV) on the way to Emmaus, seven miles from Jerusalem. They were debriefing in light of the news that Jesus's tomb had been found empty, a fact that had been investigated and confirmed by other disciples.

Wesley's best antidote was to stay as close to scripture as possible and participate in holy conferencing through the community's use of reason, tradition, and experience to interpret scripture.

The risen Jesus "drew near" to these men and joined in the conversation. Frustrated by their slowness to grasp what had happened, what does Jesus do? Does he say, "Hey! It is I! Let your own eyes (experience) be your proof"? No. Rather than directing them to rely on their experience of him, Jesus does a very Wesleyan thing, anachronistically speaking. He points them to scripture as the most accurate evidence on what has occurred. Then agreeing to stay with them in Emmaus, Jesus anchors their reasoned review of scripture and personal experience in a type of meal that would become traditional and sacramental. This is the quadrilateral in its purest form. If only Jesus could personally lead all such discussions!

25

Questions for Discussion

1. Is it possible for a person to interpret anything with complete objectivity? Why or why not?

2. Are there other sources of tradition used to interpret the scriptures that you would add to Wesley's list? If so, what are they and why would you give them special authority?

3. Why is experience dangerous as a tool of spiritual interpretation?

4. What is the relationship between Christian experience and scripture?

5. What did Wesley mean by the question: For how can a sense of our having received pardon be the condition of our receiving it?

6. How do you respond to Abraham and Wright's concerns about misusing the quadrilateral?

7. In the Emmaus Road story why didn't Jesus just let the experience of his presence suffice for supporting his resurrection?

Belief #3

Grace Is the Necessary Glue of All Discipleship

One of my wife's great-grandfathers, Chestnut Flanders, was a Rebel captain in the Civil War. That intrigued me when I first heard about "Grandpa Chess," as he is called. But that fact would not explain who Chess Flanders was or why among earlier-generation relatives he remains a topic of conversation in my wife's family. Chess Flanders was also a Methodist preacher. Late in his life people would stand outside his bedroom window to hear him bring a word from the Lord. But beyond that, Chess Flanders was a man of prayer. What has planted him firmly in the soul of my wife's family was his regular practice of praying for the next four generations into the future, that God would call many of his descendants into the Christian ministry. My ninety-year-old father-in-law was the fruit of those prayers. In his generation the annual family reunion was held on Thanksgiving Day (not on a weekend) because the great majority of those involved were either in full-time ministry, married to someone in full-time ministry, or deeply committed laypeople. You cannot understand that family without knowing about Grandpa Chess.

To understand John Wesley's life and practice it is necessary to grasp the way in which he understood the grace of God to function in a human life. The big picture of God's deployment of grace is the only explanation for the great expectations Wesley maintained for humankind.

27

We will look at two basic functions of grace without which the rest of his proclamation of scriptural Christianity cannot be properly understood.

God's Plan Is Able People—God's Grace Makes Us Able

The first of these big-picture issues can be found in the writings of Wesley scholar Randy Maddox. In his major study of Wesley's theology, *Responsible Grace*, Maddox concludes that Wesley's understanding of the scripture way of salvation has an observable core of God's gracious activity in Jesus Christ from which all else flows. He speaks of this core as Wesley's "orienting concern." Put simply, God has designed us to meaningfully, responsibly interact on our own behalf in the world. We are intended to be active, not passive, participants in the life of faith. God gives us grace to enable this responsible action. He calls this synergy "responsible grace."[1]

Maddox derives Wesley's basic orienting perspective as the product of the "vital tension" between two co-definitive truths of Christianity. "Without God's grace we *cannot* be saved; while without our (grace empowered, but uncoerced) participation, God's grace *will not* save."[2] Read that again if you need to.

We are intended to be active, not passive, participants in the life of faith. God gives us grace to enable this responsible action.

Immediately we can note that such a view of Christianity sees humankind as helpless to either rescue itself from God's judgment or restore to itself the capacities needed for faithful living. At the same time

28

we also observe in Wesley's thinking God's default determination to allow/require our participation (made possible by grace) in the enterprise of following Jesus Christ. This sounds like the makings of a spiritual oxymoron.

All Christian traditions are built around some kind of orienting concern(s) regarding how humankind ultimately is restored to fellowship with God. Wesley's view of God's grace is one among a variety of interpretations of how God engages with people. Maddox offers a review with regard to Western Christianity:

> The dominating concern of the Lutheran reformation was to emphasize the unmerited nature of justifying grace, or *free grace*. While the Reformed tradition agreed with this basic Lutheran claim, the more distinctive concern of the Reformed tradition has been to stress God's sovereign disposal of all grace, or *sovereign grace*. A direct reaction to this emphasis emerged within the Reformed tradition—the Arminian insistence on *cooperant grace*.[3]

The common denominator in all of these theological understandings is the necessity of God's grace in human salvation. The Western (Latin/Roman Catholic) church interpreted the need of humankind more in terms of guilt and absolution (referred to as the *juridical* emphasis). The Eastern (Greek/Orthodox) church interpreted the need of humankind in terms of the healing or restoration of our sinful nature (referred to as the *therapeutic* emphasis).

In any description of the influence of God's grace on human lives, the role of God and the role of people has to be delineated. Does God, must God, act unilaterally due either to God's absolute sovereignty or because of human corruption and spiritual lifelessness? If we are "like a dead person because of the things [we] did wrong and [our] offenses against God" (Eph 2:1), is there any reasonable way in which we can, thinking of Maddox's term, be responsible, even necessary *cooperant* participants in our salvation? If you were "like a dead person," how did you come to cooperate with God in your salvation?

Prevenient Grace: God Enabled Response-Ability

This question will be addressed at greater length in the next chapter. For now it can be noted that Wesley did arrive at a scriptural answer by which he navigated the theological minefield of his belief in the reality of natural human spiritual impotence. He turned to a focus on "prevenience," that is the gracious activity of God in human life *before* we know it. The word is from Latin roots meaning to "come before." The term "preventing" is used indicating a prior opening (venting) of a way for God to make possible human response. Wesley writes:

> For allowing that all the souls of men are dead by nature, this excuses none, seeing there is no man that is in a state of mere nature; there is no man, unless he has quenched the Spirit, that is wholly void of the grace of God. No man living is entirely destitute of what is vulgarly called natural conscience. But this is not natural: It is more properly termed, *preventing* grace.... Every one, unless he be one of the small number whose conscience is seared as with a hot iron, feels more or less uneasy when he acts contrary to the light of his own conscience. So that no man sins because he has not grace, but because he does not use the grace which he hath.[4]

Prior to any awareness of what God is doing, grace is given to us. One manifestation of this was spoken of in the eighteenth century as "natural conscience."[5] As Wesley affirms, this is not natural. It is "before we know it" grace that points us toward the desire to walk with God. When we "use the grace we have" and turn to God for help, Wesley believed that a spiritual chain reaction could continue from repentance to saving faith to holiness. Prevenient grace, properly understood, removes any misunderstanding that our ability to respond comes from natural human ability. It explains how lifeless sinners have the possibility of participation in a new responsible life in Christ.

> *Prior to any awareness of what God is doing, grace is given to us. This explains how lifeless sinners have the possibility of participation in a new responsible life in Christ.*

In Wesley's lifetime this "orienting concern" involved serious conflict with other Christian leaders, including his friend from Oxford days and early leader of the revival, George Whitefield. The idea that we are responsible agents in our salvation may sound innocent enough today, but in a culture where Calvinism was dominant it was highly controversial. Any suggestion of the necessity of human partnership was condemned as commending works righteousness. In 1770, the year of Whitefield's death, the published *Minutes* of the 1770 Methodist conference openly spoke of good works as indirectly essential to salvation. In the words of Wesley scholar William Abraham, "All hell broke loose."[6] For the next decade there was open rancor between the Methodists and Calvinists.

Wesley's orienting concern of responsible grace had in its core a concern for the loss of motivation on the part of Christians who saw themselves as passive recipients of mercy. Wesley saw lazy Christians all around him, unengaged because they saw no need for active engagement with the God who had, in their understanding, saved them without any activity on their part.

In spite of the very real stresses of fighting this battle, Wesley refused to forsake his understanding of how God enables/requires people to receive salvation and holiness. Did Wesley really believe in works righteousness? Do we have to add our efforts to Christ's sacrifice and the Holy Spirit's gracious endowments? We will consider that further in subsequent chapters. But one approach to an answer is found in another possible orienting concern offered by Wesley scholar Gregory Clapper.

31

The Renewal of the Heart by Grace

One of the most appealing dynamics of John Wesley's conjunctive thinking is the synthesis of "the warm heart" (piety) and "the outstretched hand" (mercy). This synthesis, however, like all of Wesley's conjunctive conclusions, calls for careful interpretation to properly understand the role of grace. Wesley was firmly committed to letting God be God. Salvation in all its dimensions is a gift of grace.

While it may seem potentially contradictory to what is about to be affirmed, let's clearly note again that Wesley was unrelenting in his insistence that righteous works follow the new birth and the receipt of the righteousness of Christ by faith. In his sermon "The Law Established through Faith, II" we read, "Thou shalt love thy neighbor as thyself. Neither is love content with barely working no evil to our neighbor. It continually incites us to do good: as we have time and opportunity, to do good in every possible kind and in every possible degree to all men."[7]

When a person follows Christ it should show. Like a tea bag lowered into hot water, what (and Who) is inside will be clearly revealed through a believer's daily life. Such a result is the *evidence*, not the cause, of salvation. Wesley believed in the inevitability of such proof for those who practiced faith in Jesus Christ. This reflexive expression of faith in outward manifestations fits in with the idea of responsible, enabling grace as an orienting concern.

Maddox, though he considers it unlikely, allows that a thinker could have more than one orienting concern.[8] Clapper makes a case for a second such basic orientation and suggests that this second concept is closer to Wesley's vision of human renewal than responsible grace. His observation is that "the renewal of the heart" can be understood as identifying the core, the "main thing," of Wesley's spirituality.

What Is Primary: Outward Evidence or Inward Change?

Once again we observe in Wesley's beliefs an appreciation of the reality that in relationships more than one thing can be true at the same time, but true in relationship to other truths. This reality is illustrated in his sermon "The Scripture Way of Salvation" (1765). Comparing and contrasting the place of faith and works in salvation, he speaks of them as not being necessary "in the same sense" and not "in the same degree."

> But they [results of repentance] are not necessary in the *same sense* with faith, nor in the *same degree*. Not in the *same degree*; for those fruits are only necessary *conditionally*, if there be time and opportunity for them. Otherwise a man may be justified without them, as was the "thief" upon the cross.... But he cannot be justified without faith: this is impossible. Likewise let a man have ever so much repentance, or ever so many of the fruits meet for repentance, yet all this does not at all avail: he is not justified till he believes. But the moment he believes, with or without those fruits, yea, with more or less repentance, he is justified.[9]

Works are for Wesley "necessary" *conditionally* as evidence of the presence of saving/sanctifying grace in a human life. Such a "test" was not for the sake of self-congratulation or supplementing God's grace. This calling for evidentiary behavior was a protection against one of sin's most common, though less frequently apprehended, manifestations: self-delusion.

Works are for Wesley "necessary" conditionally as evidence of the presence of saving/sanctifying grace in a human life.

First John 3:17-18 reads: "If a person has material possessions and sees a brother or sister in need and that person doesn't care—how can the love of God remain in him? Little children, let's not love with words or speech but with action and truth." Commenting on the question of verse 17, "how can the love of God remain in him?" Wesley concludes, "Certainly not at all, however he may talk (verse 18) of loving God."[10] Wesley did not want anyone to be deluded by the ability to "talk the talk" of Christian doctrine and/or experience apart from faith engaged with real life. It is altogether possible to fool oneself into believing that an intellectual understanding of salvation is sufficient. This possibility is especially real to those who preach or teach.

In a culture where many were baptized as infants, a culture strongly influenced by Calvinistic theology that militantly resisted any appearance of human merit in salvation, Wesley constantly contended against a kind of autopilot Christianity. Grace, he repeatedly declared, made a believer "responsible" for "action and truth," as 1 John 3:18 puts it. This, Maddox clearly illustrates, was an orienting concern, a main thing never to be forgotten.

Sometimes the remedy for one problem can create another. So it was for Wesley's commitment to the necessity of human response to grace. As the Calvinists had protested, this position regarding "works" did incline some Methodists to pride. Wesley, in a letter to John Newton, stated, "I think on Justification just as I have done any time these seven-and-twenty years, and just as Mr. Calvin does. In this respect I do not differ from him a hair's breadth."[11] Seeking to properly relate unmerited grace on which he and Calvin agreed to an expectation of human response led Wesley to clarify the relationship of the inner experience of grace to an outer expression in a believer's life. He speaks to the nuances of his understanding of grace and works in a letter to "John Smith" in 1745. Wesley warned, "I would rather say faith is 'productive of all Christian *holiness*,' than 'of all Christian *practice*'; because men are so exceeding apt to rest in 'practice,' so called, I mean *outside religion*;

whereas *true religion* is eminently seated in the heart, renewed in the image of him that created us" (emphasis in original).[12]

His ministry was constantly punctuated with concern for the potentially deadening effects of an incorrect preoccupation with either an inward or outward focus in the Christian life. He challenged, for example, overly pious persons who emphasized inward "stillness" and likewise, as we have just read, offered correction to those for whom "practice" was dominant.

Works Without Heart Are Dead

In this ongoing tug-of-war, it is clear that his ultimate priority was to protect as well as clearly proclaim the necessity of God's gracious initiative as the foundation of all faith and practice. The arena where this divine initiative and sanctifying purpose take root and grow is within the heart. The "heart" for Wesley was our human capacity for self-determination, a capacity aided by God's grace. He referred to this capacity, which he most often spoke of, as "affections." This means much more than feelings, but speaks of the competency of the Spirit-enabled will.

The heart is where our mission and motivation as human beings begins. We hear this in Wesley's sermon "The Way to the Kingdom":

> Yea, two persons may do the same outward work—suppose, feeding the hungry, or clothing the naked—and in the meantime one of these may be truly religious and the other have no religion at all; for the one may act from the love of God, and the other from the love of praise. So manifest is it that although true religion naturally leads to every good word and work, yet the real nature thereof lies deeper still, even in the "Hidden man of the heart."[13]

Two scripture passages immediately come to mind:

> Above all else, guard your heart, everything you do flows from it. (Prov 4:23 NIV)

The kingdom of God is in your midst. (Luke 17:21 NIV)

In the *Interpreters Bible,* commenting on Jesus's words in Luke 17, George Buttrick writes, "It follows that the kingdom is within, but only because it has first entered the world in Jesus: the kingdom spreads by the new nature which Christ's own receive through him, and that nature is the only progress."[14]

And Maddox observes that Wesley "repeatedly insisted that the essence of sanctification was not mere outward conformity to law, but the renewal of our affections (heart) through participation in the Divine nature."[15]

What we are hearing Wesley declare is that neither *orthodoxy*, right thinking/knowing nor *orthopraxy*, right doing, suffice as the core of Christian spirituality. We might recall Jesus's words in Matthew 7:21-23:

> Not everybody who says to me, "Lord, Lord," will get into the kingdom of heaven. Only those who do the will of my Father who is in heaven will enter. On the Judgment Day, many people will say to me, "Lord, Lord, didn't we prophesy in your name and expel demons in your name and do lots of miracles in your name?" Then I'll tell them, "I've never known you. Get away from me, you people who do wrong."

Consider also the words of the Apostle Paul in 1 Corinthians 13:

> If I speak in tongues of human beings and of angels but I don't have love, I'm a clanging gong or a clashing cymbal. If I have the gift of prophesy and I know all the mysteries and everything else, and if I have such complete faith that I can move mountains but I don't have love, I'm nothing. If I give away everything that I have and hand over my own body to feel good about what I've done but I don't have love, I receive no benefit whatsoever. (vv. 1–3)

Clapper has coined a third term to express what it is both Jesus and Paul are affirming as necessary for true righteousness. He speaks of *orthocardia* or a right heart.[16] Wesley scholar Theodore Runyon employs a term with complimentary implications: *orthopathy* or right "feelings, affections, and in the larger sense, *experience*."[17] These terms seek to give identity to the grace-assisted response of the inner person to God's grace. For Wesley this inner connection with the Spirit of God was the heart of the heart of true Christian living. In the final paragraph of his sermon "Original Sin," he proclaims, "Ye know that the great end of religion is to renew our hearts in the image of God.... Ye know that all religion which does not answer this end, all that stops short of this, the renewal of our soul in the image of God, after the likeness of him that created it, is in no other than a poor farce and a mere mockery of God, to the destruction of our own soul."[18]

The terms orthocardia (right heart) and orthopathy (right feelings) seek to give identity to the grace-assisted response of the inner person to God's grace.

Does this negate or conflict with Wesley's burden for outward demonstration, for social or communal fellowship? To the contrary, these are examples of conjunctive thinking based on a clear and prior understanding that the cause of outward demonstration and corporate faith development is the inner influence and empowerment in the human heart by God's grace. In a letter to John Valton (1771) Wesley writes, "The most prevailing fault among the Methodists is to be *too outward* in religion. We are continually forgetting that the kingdom of God is *within* us."[19] This is a matter of keeping first things first as well as a pastoral check against pride. This is a concern within a concern, the place of the heart within the action of God's grace.

Salvation: A Bird with Two Wings

In the "common English translation" used by Wesley in his *Explanatory Notes Upon the New Testament*, James 1:27 (KJV) identifies

37

"pure religion" with these words: "Pure religion and undefiled before God even the Father is this, To visit the fatherless and widows in their affection, *and* to keep himself unspotted from the world."[20] In his notes on this verse Wesley affirms James's clear connection between "true religion" and works of mercy along with moral purity. "The only true *religion* in the sight of God is *this, to visit*—With Counsel, comfort and relief. *The Fatherless and widows*—Those who need it most. *In their affliction*—In their most helpless and hopeless state. *And to keep himself unspotted from the world*—from the maxims, tempers, and customs of it."[21]

Compassionate and pure behavior (true religion) in the life of a follower of Jesus Christ is like the flavors and colors that inevitably steep from tea when it is lowered into boiling water. The agitated waters of human need have a way of releasing the loving presence of Christ in those living a life of true Christian faith. James's words are the epicenter of scripture in witnesses to the inescapable link between faith and works. Wesley echoes this witness. But…in the chicken and egg relationship of faith and works Wesley returns to the necessity of *orthocardia* (right heart). Concluding his comments on James 1:27 he immediately adds, "But this (true religion) cannot be done till we have given our hearts to God…."[22]

In Philippians 2, having exalted Jesus Christ in the great hymn of verses 5-11, the Apostle Paul writes, "Therefore…carry out your own salvation with fear and trembling. God is the one who enables you both to want and to actually live out his good purposes." God takes the initiative in renewing our hearts so that we can engage life as the arena in which we work out the relationship between faith and works. It takes both wings, faith and works, to move a disciple forward in living out the mind that was in Christ Jesus.

To seek to understand and apply the merest of Wesley's doctrinal priorities does not mean searching for simplistic conclusions. It means:

- the discipline that should be second nature to a disciple;
- the work implied in "working out our salvation";
- the depth of love called for in loving God with all of our heart and soul and mind and our neighbor as ourselves;
- the unwillingness to any longer be conformed to the pattern of this world;
- a desire to be transformed with a renewed mind that can test and approve what God's will is;
- a longing for an enlightening of the eyes of the heart in order to know the hope to which we have been called;
- all of which is summed up in having this mind in you that was in Christ Jesus.
- This is the dynamic of grace in the life of a holy warrior.

It begins and continues under the impulse of God's grace in the heart; by the light of the scripture interpreted through reason, experience, and tradition, it grows as the affections within prompt response in the world.

In the chapters that follow, the core elements of repentance, faith, and holiness will be considered. The goal is not just a better understanding of Wesley's thought. Knowledge can sometimes promote pride. The goal is strengthening the foundation for discipleship. In *The Renewal of the Heart Is the Mission of the Church*, Gregory Clapper observes that these three doctrines "are key not only, or even primarily because they are 'distinctively Methodist'... but because they are *most important for the foundational formation of disciples*. Because they are *indispensably formative of the heart* is most likely the reason they *became* distinctively Methodist.[23]

Contemporary British evangelist Ian Leitch declares, "We are not in Christianity to get an A+ in theology—did you know that? We are in Christianity to get an A+ in being conformed to the image of Jesus Christ."[24] Wesley would heartily agree. With this purpose clearly in mind we will continue to study Wesley's perspectives and pursue an A+ in being conformed to the image of Christ beginning with repentance.

Questions for Discussion

1. Why would human cooperation with God in our salvation be so controversial?

2. How have you cooperated with God in your salvation?

3. What does it mean to say that works are the evidence and not the cause of salvation?

4. What does it mean for the kingdom of God to be within us?

5. Why did Wesley understand the renewal of the heart as our primary need?

6. What is the difference in seeking to get an A+ in theology and seeking to be conformed to the image of Jesus Christ?

Prevenient Grace: God Takes the Initiative

A standard old church joke goes as follows:

"I went to church today."

"What did the preacher talk about?"

"Sin."

"What did he say?"

"He's against it."

As a United Methodist pastor in the twenty-first century I can confidently say addressing the subject of sin in the so-called postmodern world rarely seems that cut and dried. But that is not as new of a situation as one might think. Consider this complaint of a traditional Christian:

> The tendency of modern thought is to reject dogmas, creeds, and every kind of bounds in religion. It is thought grand and wise to condemn no opinion whatsoever, and to pronounce all earnest and clever teachers to be trustworthy.... Everything forsooth is true, and nothing is false! Everybody is right, and nobody is wrong! Everybody is likely to be saved, and nobody is to be lost! The atonement and substitution of Christ, the personality of the devil, the miraculous element in Scripture, the reality and eternity of future punishment, all these mighty foundation stones are cooly tossed overboard, like lumber, in order to lighten the ship of Christianity

41

and enable it to keep pace with modern science. Stand up for these great verities, and you are called narrow, illiberal, old-fashioned, and a theological fossil! Quote a text, and you are told that all truth is not confined to the pages of an ancient Jewish Book, and that free inquiry has found out many things since the Book was completed.[1]

This was written by Anglican Bishop J. C. Ryle...in 1877! With a little tweaking of terms it might have been penned yesterday. Controversy over the nature of sin has been brewing since before John Wesley was born. The study of Christian theology and doctrine in the centuries since might be compared to the experience of famed movie actress Mae West who quipped, "I used to be Snow White—but I drifted."[2] As Christian doctrines "drifted" in modern times, secular visions of human dysfunction arose to compete with traditional thinking. Freud, looking within human nature, found alienation from self. Marx, seeing human dysfunction as a corporate matter, challenged humankind's understanding of its political nature. The ironic result of these evolutions in thought has been the postmodern world, increasingly inclined to moral subjectivity, like Adam and Eve, wanting to reset or reject inherited moral standards.

It would be an understatement to say that John Wesley took the subject of sin seriously. He considered the "fallen" state of every human being a part of the gospel story that could not be removed without rendering the entire work of salvation pointless. Let me ask you: When was the last time you heard a sermon on the subject of original sin? How did we get from Wesley's intense proclamation of this doctrine to today? What did original sin mean to Wesley? How did he understand God's method of enabling hopelessly fallen people to re-engage with the holy God?

It's the Enlightenment, Stupid!

Some may remember one of the themes of Bill Clinton's first presidential campaign. "It's the economy, stupid!" That was an oversimplication for the sake of communication, as are most such slogans. As we begin to think about "original sin," allow me to employ an oversimplified slogan that Wesley might have plastered around Great Britain and is still relevant today: "It's the Enlightenment, stupid!" Of course, the main problem with this as a slogan for Wesley is that the term "Enlightenment" did not begin to be used until about one hundred years after Wesley died. Okay. Just the same, the general period of time (1650–1800) during which John Wesley's parents and their children (including John and Charles) lived, paralleled what is now called the Enlightenment or the Age of Reason. Wesley felt the effects of the Enlightenment in a limited way. Centuries later it impacts our thinking every day.

Remembering the terms of the quadrilateral, for hundreds of years leading up to the Protestant Reformation in the 1500s, the primary source of authority in Western Christianity had been *tradition*. The Roman Catholic Church, a tradition-laden institution, ruled. During the Reformation years, 1500–1650, there was a resurgence of *scripture* as a voice of authority, with Calvin and Luther seeking to reform church tradition and bring it in line with the Bible. Beginning in Wesley's day in the 1700s, *reason*, slowly infiltrating culture with a suspicion of the supernatural and an emphasis on science, became a prominent voice of authority into the 1800s and far beyond. In the later part of the nineteenth century in philosophy and literature there was a renewed interest in *experience* as a primary way of determining values. For centuries information and the authority it conveys was controlled by whoever was in power. Only the verdict of history will determine the most influential voices of authority in the crazy quilt of our information-rich twenty-first century.

New Testament scholar N. T. Wright concludes, "Much of what has been written about the Bible in the last two hundred years has either been following through the Enlightenment's program, or reacting to it, or negotiating some kind of halfway house in between."[3] The journey to the diversity of opinion about morals we experience in the twenty-first century has been long and convoluted, but unrelenting. A telling observation by American philosopher Alan Bloom, at the time teaching at the University of Chicago, captures the extent of the drift from scripture to self as the final source of authority. Looking at American culture as the twentieth century was ending, he wrote, "we do not love a thing because it is good, it is good because we love it."[4] Wesley would surely see this outcome as an entirely logical consequence of original sin as the scriptures portray it. Rising confidence in the power of reason by the educated classes (later paralleled by willingness to attribute authority to experience) accelerated what Wesley saw in the doctrine of original sin as humankind's native self-authorizing bent.

For Wesley Original Sin Was Watercooler Subject Matter

Consider this as an icebreaker in a small group: What's the worst sin you ever committed? I've actually started with that question, just to watch the reaction for a moment. No one has ever come close to objecting that they have never sinned. Of course, we go on to something more agreeable, but in the space of two or three seconds it usually becomes clear that human sinfulness is universal.

That humanity is "foolish and sinful, fallen short of the glorious image of God" was an essential conviction of John Wesley.[5] Although this emphasis was not a part of the historic creeds, he understood it as foundational to Christian belief. The origin of such corruption was the "fall" from grace of our ancient parents. This doctrine was a familiar part of the Church of England's *Thirty-nine Articles*. Article Nine declares, "Original sin...is the fault and corruption of the Nature of every man, that naturally is engendered of the offspring of Adam; whereby man is very far gone from original righteousness, and is of his own nature inclined to evil, so that the flesh lusteth contrary to the spirit; and therefore in every person born into this world, it deserveth God's wrath and damnation."[6]

Popular Christian author and Presbyterian pastor John Ortberg writes that his wife created a bumper sticker related to original sin, though no one would likely guess the connection. The sticker was based on the comedy of British comedian Eddie Izzard. Eddie tells of growing up in a little church and hearing about the doctrine of original sin. However, he was a bit fuzzy on the concept. He assumed it meant priests got tired of hearing the same old boring confessions, so they wanted somebody who would confess to an original—or new—sin.

Instead of the old standbys such as greed and lust, Eddie came up with a sin no one had ever confessed before: "I poke badgers with spoons." John Ortberg's wife was so struck with its originality she had a bumper sticker made and put it on her car!

Ortberg, seeking to help explain the concept's meaning, goes on to note a classic response to original sin was made by a fourth-century monk named Pelagius. Pelagius differed with the understanding of original sin promoted by his contemporary Augustine. The Augustinian view held original sin to be fundamental moral failure transmitted from generation to generation. Pelagius believed human beings are blank slates at the time of birth, potentially innocent. Ortberg quips, "Pelagius clearly never had children."[7]

In his sermon "Original Sin" (1759), Wesley refers to Genesis 6:5, "God saw that the wickedness of man was great in the earth, and that every imagination of the thoughts of his heart was *only* evil continually" (KJV).[8] At the end of the first section of the sermon, he places a verbal exclamation mark on the radical nature of human lostness by affirming, "it was always the same, that it 'was only evil *continually*'—every year, every day, every hour, every moment. He (humankind) never deviated into good."[9] In this same sermon he affirms, "Is man by nature filled with all manner of evil? Is he void of all good? Is he wholly fallen? Is his soul totally corrupted? Or, to come back to the text, is 'every imagination of the thoughts of his heart evil continually?' Allow this, and you are so far a Christian. Deny it, and you are an heathen still."[10]

45

Wesley the evangelist and spiritual director was convinced sinners would not embrace the therapy of God's grace in Jesus Christ until they understood the extent to which they were hopelessly degraded with the corruption of unrighteousness.

If you have read classic British literature you are aware eighteenth-century England was firmly in the grip of a social system where the idea of equality among all people was virtually unknown. British evangelicals like Whitefield and Wesley were profoundly radical, in the truest sense of the word, in their proclamation of this doctrine. Having heard George Whitefield proclaim this universal need for God's mercy, the Duchess of Buckingham complained to her upper-class peer, the Countess of Huntington:

> I thank your ladyship for the information concerning Methodist preachers. Their doctrines are most repulsive and strongly tinctured with impertinence and disrespect towards their superiors, in perpetually endeavoring to level all ranks and do away with all distinctions. It is monstrous to be told that you have a heart as sinful as the common wretches that crawl the earth.[11]

Monstrous though it may seem to aristocrats, this was exactly Wesley's belief. Scholar Thomas Oden writes that Wesley perceived the doctrine of original sin as "the only Christian doctrine supported by extensive empirical evidence."[12] N. T. Wright has written, "Part of the Christian story . . . is that human beings have been so seriously damaged by evil that what they need isn't simply better self-knowledge, or better social conditions, but help, and indeed rescue, from outside themselves."[13] Wesley was convinced that every individual comes into the world possessed of an inherited disposition to unrighteousness and in need of such rescue.

Prevenient Grace: The Unseen Gift of God

Obviously Wesley and his fellow Methodist preachers proclaimed human lostness with fervor. So how did Wesley square human depravity with salvation by grace, human participation, and the message of salvation offered to all?

Even as God is preparing to banish Adam and Eve from the garden it is clear that the Creator has a remedy for disobedience. God creates garments to bring the beginnings of civilizing grace to this new chapter in the human story (Gen 3:21). Such primitive clothing is a powerful foreshadowing of future provisions of mercy: "All of you who were baptized into Christ have clothed yourselves with Christ" (Gal 3:27). The Apostle Paul would one day write of God's answer to sin in Jesus Christ, "Where sin increased, grace multiplied even more" (Rom 5:20). As important as original sin was to Wesley's scriptural Christianity, apart from such original love there would be no gospel of amazing grace.

In a broad sense, Wesleyan thinkers use the term *prevenience* ("come before") to identify this proactive provision of grace. Like a battery in a car, prevenient grace sparks the engine of faith. In every dimension of salvation, the actions of God through grace occur preveniently, initially before we know it, and continually after we have awakened, thus enabling continued growth in grace. Wesley would have seen this broad view of God's saving initiative in Article X of the Anglican *Thirty-nine Articles of Religion*:

> The condition of Man after the fall of Adam is such, that he cannot turn and prepare himself, by his own natural strength and good works, to faith, and calling upon God. Wherefore we have no power to do good works pleasant and acceptable to God, without the grace of God by Christ preventing us, that we many have a good will, and working with us, when we have this good will.[14]

The primary scriptural basis for prevenient grace is John 1:9, "The true light that shines on all people was coming into the world." For Wesley, this universal blessing of grace provided a solution to the problems of (1) how *all* persons could have the possibility of responding in faith and, (2) how all persons *though sinful in nature* could be enabled to respond to God's offer of salvation.

It is generally true that Wesleyan theology teaches "free will" in comparison to those Calvinists who hold that some are elected for salvation and others are not. But in point of fact, Wesley did not teach what is commonly understood as free will. In the *Minutes* of the 1745 Annual Conference, Wesley describes Methodist teaching as coming up to "the very edge of Calvinism" by: "(1.) . . . ascribing all good to the free grace of God. (2.) In denying all natural free-will, and all power antecedent to grace. And (3.) In excluding all merit from man; even for what he has or does by the grace of God."[15]

What Wesley actually taught was not free will but free/cooperant grace. This specifically begins with prevenient grace that infuses light into every person. In his sermon "Free Grace," he describes it as "free in all and free for all."[16] Again, in "On Working Out Our Own Salvation," he affirms:

> For allowing that all souls of men are dead in sin by *nature*, this excuses none, seeing there is no man that is in a state of mere nature; there is no man, unless he has quenched the Spirit, that is wholly void of the grace of God. No man living is entirely destitute of what is vulgarly called "natural conscience." But this is not natural; it is more properly termed "preventing grace." . . . Everyone has some measure of that light, some faint glimmering ray, which sooner or later, more or less, enlightens every man that cometh into the world.[17]

God's loving energy does not forsake us. Grace enables every person to have a measure of choice. No person, as Wesley understands it, is in a purely "natural," graceless condition.

> *No person, as Wesley understands it, is in a purely "natural," graceless condition.*

A primary function of grace in this restraining role is the work of conscience, which we have just heard Wesley qualify as "not natural" but "more properly termed 'preventing grace.'" Wesley affirmed this in his sermon "On Conscience":

> Can it be denied that something of this is found in every man born into the world? And does it not appear as soon as the understanding opens, as soon as reason begins to dawn? Does not every one then begin to know that there is a difference between good and evil; how imperfect soever the various circumstances of this sense of good and evil may be?...This faculty seems to be what is usually meant by those who speak of natural conscience; an expression frequently found in some of our best authors, but yet not strictly just. For though in one sense it may be termed natural, because it is found in all men; yet properly speaking, it is not natural, but a supernatural gift of God, above all his natural endowments. No; it is not nature, but the Son of God, that is "the true light, which enlighteneth every man that cometh into the world."[18]

Prevenient Grace—Stir Up the Gift That Is Within You

What does prevenient grace do in human lives? Prevenient grace moves in a human life to bring fresh sensitivity to the conscience. Such grace also brings a degree of strength to the human will, both to possess some degree of freedom of choice and power over evil.

It might immediately be objected these characteristics are not obvious in everyone. That is clearly true. The benefits of prevenient grace can be diminished both by our failure to stir up this grace and by ungracious influences, discouraging or suppressing our appropriation of grace. What is essential to understand is Wesley understood the grace of God to be the source of human response-ability.

When I meet with parents to discuss the baptism of their children, one of my primary goals is to introduce or elaborate on the subject of prevenient grace. I encourage them they/he/she will be among God's primary instruments in the engagement of their child with the grace of

God. The "home" is intended to be an incubator of faith, opening the door to grace.

Wesley understood the grace of God to be the source of human response-ability.

For better or worse, the initial influence of God can be maximized or minimized in training (or discouraging) "children in the way they should go" (Prov 22:6). How early does this begin? I think of one man I know who was seriously neglected until he was removed from his home of origin at the age of three and placed with a Christian family. While it was later obvious during his adolescent years the Spirit of God was striving in his life, he is now nearing retirement age and is still estranged from God.

What about you? Have you understood and can you discern the before-you-were-ever-aware-of-it activity of God in your life? In Philippians 1:6 the Apostle Paul, speaking of God, says, "The one who started a good work in you." Has it dawned on you that God began a good work in you long before you knew it?

A Personal Testimony

There is no explanation for my life apart from prevenient grace. As a boy I lived down the street from the Methodist church in a small northern Indiana town. Members of our family were not regular attendees of worship, but somewhere along the way I was given a tiny book called *The Little Bible*. It contained the Beatitudes, the Apostles' Creed, and the Ten Commandments. I don't remember reading it but I carried it in my pants pocket every day. It went through the laundry more than once. In my child's mind it somehow symbolized the reality of God.

At the age of eight I began taking guitar lessons. I never became a great player but I learned a few chords. I remember sitting in my bedroom, playing and singing "The Old Rugged Cross." Obviously it had stuck in my mind from our rare visits to church. Somehow it struck a different kind of chord deep within me, though I did not understand it.

We moved just south of Indianapolis when I was eleven, living in a country subdivision. Other than an Easter or two, church was not part of my life. Those were hard years in my parents' marriage, and I feared they would divorce. I began praying the Lord's Prayer at night when I got in bed. As time passed I would pray myself asleep with the words "Thy will be done." I had tried everything I could think of to bring peace at home and had come to the conclusion God knew best and I would put it in his hands.

Early in my high school years my parents and I went to see the movie version of *The Greatest Story Ever Told*. In the story when they took John the Baptist out to behead him I found myself asking, "Do I believe in God enough to die for my faith?" It was not long afterward that a call to the pastoral ministry welled up within me, though I really had almost no idea what that meant. I told my parents, who were "God fearing" but not Christ-centered people, about it. They did not discourage me, probably thinking it would soon be forgotten. It was not. When I eventually got a driver's license, I began going to a United Methodist church with a cousin of mine whose family also did not attend church. I eventually told the pastor about my call and he was encouraging, though he must have wondered how it came to be.

At my high school graduation I gave one of the speeches. A man there to take our pictures as we received our diplomas was impressed with my speech and offered me a job shooting fall public school pictures. I would then go to college the rest of the year. It was a good-paying job so I said yes. I had planned to attend a state school but with this job on the horizon I went through the many college catalogs I had written for the previous year. Some of them had the word "Methodist" associated with them. One, a small Christian college (I had no idea what that meant), was not too expensive, offered Greek (which I somehow thought I needed), and was on the quarter system rather than semesters. That seemed like it would work better with my job situation. I had never heard of this school but it was accredited so I applied and ended up there the week after Christmas, having worked in the fall.

The day I arrived there was a terrible snowstorm. Many students could not get back. On New Year's Eve I went to a late-night worship service at which they used the John Wesley covenant service. I had never heard of John Wesley and barely knew what a covenant was. At the conclusion of the service I waited to take communion and had an experience unlike any I had ever known. It was like a voice within said, *I am here and I am alive.* In the days that followed something was different. There in that strongly Christian environment, when I heard the name of Jesus it was like hearing about someone I had met. That was my Aldersgate experience, not dramatic or emotional, but one that set my life in a new direction. God had been at work in my life and I had not recognized it. At last I began to wake up to God's presence in a personal way.

Both Jesus's words in Revelation 3 about knocking on our door and the simple affirmation of 1 John 4:19, "We love him because he first loved us," illustrate the divine initiative God has taken in Jesus Christ. God, not us, began the good work in us. Before we ever know it, the Savior has begun to provide the conditions that make our search for God, who is actually seeking us, possible.

Questions for Discussion

1. How do you respond to the evaluation of contemporary society: "We do not love a thing because it is good; it is good because we love it"?

2. Wesley was convinced that sinners would not embrace the therapy of God's grace in Jesus Christ until they understood they were naturally corrupted with unrighteousness. Do you agree with Wesley's view? Why?

3. Thomas Oden says that original sin is "the only Christian doctrine supported by empirical evidence." What does he mean? Do you agree or disagree?

4. In his sermon "On Working Out Your Own Salvation" Wesley identifies basic components of the biblical discipleship pathway: prevenient grace, converting grace/repentance, justification, sanctification, pure love/the fullness of Christ. Where are you in this journey?

5. How would you describe prevenient grace?

6. What is the primary biblical text for this doctrine?

7. How would you express your gratitude for the "good work" begun in you by God?

Belief #5

Repentance: Grace Awakens Us

Wake up! That's what Jesus declared as he began his ministry. In Mark 1 we hear Jesus's invitation, "Now is the time! Here comes God's kingdom! Change your hearts and lives, and trust this good news" (v. 15). What does it mean to repent?

When, as told in the preceding chapter, I saw the movie *The Greatest Story Ever Told*, the moment I remember most clearly was when John the Baptist (played by Charlton Heston) was taken away to be executed. The actual beheading was not shown, but right before the swishing sound of the axe was heard, John's final cry echoed across the theater, "REPENT!" At the time I had absolutely no idea what that meant. But knowing that it cost John his life burned the word into my memory. God was waking me up.

At the outset of Jesus's ministry he clearly affirms that repenting would be foundational to his kingdom. "Change your hearts and lives, and trust this good news." Surely this opening declaration was the product of long, prayerful thought. The words we now read in Mark 1:15 were history's most incomparable wake-up call. What did it mean to repent and believe the good news?

Always striving to be faithful to scripture, Wesley saw that repentance was a dynamic attitude and act, conjunctive in nature, both inward and outward. He also understood there were nuances to repentance that mattered to the overall understanding of salvation. So his teaching and preaching about repentance was not simplistic. Do not let that be off-putting. To modify a familiar saying, "The angels are in the details." Wrestling with Wesley's understanding of repentance, far from an academic ordeal, is a precious opportunity to more fully engage the grace of God.

Salvation: Journey Inward—Journey Outward

In a sermon written in 1741, "Hypocrisy in Oxford," Wesley offers a list of the elements that might be experienced in the process of waking up (repentance):

1) sorrow on account of sin

2) humiliation under the hand of God

3) hatred to sin

4) confession of sin

5) ardent supplication of the divine mercy

6) the love of God

7) ceasing from sin

8) firm purpose of new obedience

9) restitution of ill-gotten goods

10) forgiving our neighbor his transgressions against us

11) good works[1]

56

These preforgiveness attitudes and actions were sometimes spoken of by Wesley as "legal" repentance. God's law has been broken. Pardon is necessary because the knowledge of sin comes through the Law. In response to God's law and the loving perfection with which it was lived out in Jesus Christ, sinners are "convinced" of their need for forgiveness and, ultimately, of the necessity of salvation by grace alone.

Wesley saw that repentance was a dynamic attitude and act, conjunctive in nature, both inward and outward.

The activity of God's grace that cultivates legal repentance is at times identified by Wesley as "convincing grace." "Twas grace that taught my heart to fear." The term "convincing grace" could suggest that this is essentially an interior process. Repentance is sometimes defined as "changing your mind." Does Wesley's list look like a collection of exclusively interior exercises? Obviously not, but for Wesley to insist on outward behaviors as part of repentance sounded to many like adding human effort to grace.

Early in my years of ministry I attended the two-week training for a through-the-Bible study, *The Bethel Bible Series.* I was given a button that said "Think Hebrew." We were warned that as a part of the Western world our modern thinking had been strongly influenced by the Greeks. One of the primary results of Greek influence had to do with understanding faith as essentially a matter of what one thinks rather than what one does. Hebrew people, that button was to remind us, did not think in such exclusively intangible ways.

A classic illustration of the difference in response is the story of a tightrope walker who had walked across a rope suspended over a deep canyon and then announced to the excited spectators gathered to watch, "I will now go back across and am going to push a wheelbarrow in front of me. Who believes I can do it?" As the story goes, many in the enthusiastic crowd waved their hands in support. Then the tightrope walker asked, "Who will ride in the wheelbarrow?"

As a practical matter, all of his ministry Wesley would aggressively contend against faith that was just talk as a breeding ground of moral laxness and tepid discipleship. Such insistence upon behaviors as evidence of repentance and faith pushed against the boarders of "works righteousness." But understanding grace through faith as conjunctively motivating inner and outer responses, changes of mind and changes of behavior, Wesley would not settle for a partial understanding of repentance. Hold that thought.

The Starting Place Is Always Grace, but Grace Is Not a Stopping Place

As observed thus far in this chapter, Wesley believed repentance as the Bible taught it was more than an inner, "spiritual" experience. He well understood the response of his critics who viewed any inclusion of "works" in human salvation as heresy. Wesley could have written their criticisms for them. He, too, was deeply concerned to guard the unparalleled role of grace in human salvation.

Wesley addresses this in his 1746 sermon "The Way to the Kingdom," based on Jesus's call to repentance in Mark 1:15.[2] He preaches that the kingdom of God "does not properly consist in any outward actions of what kind so ever," and even goes so far as to say,

> Yet may a man both abstain from outward evil, and do good, and still have no religion. Yea, two persons may do the same outward work—suppose, feeding the hungry or clothing the naked—and in the meantime one of these may be truly religious and the other have no religion at all; for the one may act from the love of God, and the other from the love of praise. So manifest it is that although true religion naturally leads to every good word and work, yet the real nature thereof lies deeper still, even "in the hidden man of the heart."[3]

Wesley was laboring to maintain the necessary relationship between "every good work" and "the real nature" of true religion, the result of the grace of God "in the hidden man of the heart."

Is this an attempt to have your cake and eat it too? No. It is the dynamic, conjunctive nature of biblical faith. St. Paul states it succinctly in Galatians 5:6, "The only thing that counts is faith expressing itself through love" (NIV).

The dynamics of grace engaged by faith begins with repentance, the spade work for the preparation of the heart.

Can you begin to appreciate the conjunction, the balance for which Wesley was constantly striving? On the one hand, like the reformers, he was committed to salvation by grace. On the other, he was equally committed to an understanding of the dynamics of grace engaged by faith that always expects human (grace-enabled) participation. This dynamic conjunction begins with repentance, the spade work for the preparation of the heart.

Repentance: Grace-Empowered Awakening

In his sermon "On Working Out Our Own Salvation," Wesley says, "Salvation is carried on by 'convincing grace,' usually in scripture termed 'repentance,' which brings a larger measure of self-knowledge, and a farther deliverance from the heart of stone."[4] Self-knowledge is an essential principle of repentance in Wesley's thinking. Awakening to self can lead to poverty of spirit, which Jesus said is blessed. Humility opens the door to faith (Matt 5:3-4).

One of Wesley's most helpful images in communicating elements of the order of salvation is his so-called "house of religion."[5] In this conception, repentance is the porch of the house, the front door is faith/justification, and the rooms of the house represent sanctification/holiness. As can be seen from the list of possible repentance behaviors/attitudes at the beginning of this chapter, this can be a large porch! The porch is the "gettin' ready" place, the time in our lives when we are awakening to the depth of our need and being prepared by grace to give up any pretense of ever earning God's mercy.

The porch is the "gettin' ready" place, the time in our lives when we are awakening to the depth of our need and being prepared by grace to give up any pretense of ever earning God's mercy.

In *Mere Christianity*, C. S. Lewis describes this process with remarkable clarity.

> No man knows how bad he is until he has tried very hard to be good.... The main thing we learn from a serious attempt to practice the Christian virtues is that we fail. If there was any idea that God has set us a sort of exam, and that we might get good marks by deserving them, that has to be wiped out.... I think that everyone who has come to some vague belief in God, until he becomes a Christian, has the idea of an exam, or of a bargain in his mind. The first result of real Christianity is to blow that idea into bits. When they find it blown into bits, some people think that means Christianity is a failure and give up. They seem to imagine that God is very simple minded. In fact, of course, He knows all about this. One of the very things Christianity was designed to do was to blow this idea to bits. God has been waiting for the moment at which you discover that there is no question of earning a pass mark in this exam.[6]

How does this process happen? That question brings us back to the subject of works, faith, and grace. As Lewis implies we will try various works in an effort to arrive at a satisfactory relationship with God. None of those works will achieve that end. However, there are works that are part of the process. They illustrate grace is at work and the will, while still in need of rebirth, is awakening. At this point such efforts are expressions of a kind of faith and the fruit of grace. Works that are part of the process of repentance have no merit to save, but they can serve as evidence of a grace-enabled desire to walk in faithfulness.

Works that are part of the process of repentance have no merit to save, but they can serve as evidence of a grace-enabled desire to walk in faithfulness.

In Acts 26 the Apostle Paul is addressing King Agrippa in Caesarea, explaining his story and message. In verses 19-20 we read, "So, King Agrippa, I wasn't disobedient to that heavenly vision....My message was that they should change their hearts and lives and turn to God, and that they should demonstrate this change in their behavior." Using King James language, Wesley would speak of such deeds as "works meet for repentance."

Repentance: A (Grace-Enabled) Fledgling Form of Faith

In his most theologically technical moments in the earlier years of the revival, Wesley would categorically reject all works done before justification as unholy. This view could be based on scripture such as Romans 14:23: "Everything that isn't based on faith is sin," and Hebrews 11:6, "It's impossible to please God without faith." His understanding of the

relationship of faith (and degrees of faith) to repentance and salvation as
well as the role of prevenient grace was still being worked out.[7] We find
a modification in Wesley's understanding in the Minutes of the 1744
Annual Conference:

> Q. 1. What is it to be justified?
> A. To be pardoned and received into God's favor and into such a
> state that, if we continue therein, we shall be finally saved.
> Q. 2. Is faith the condition of justification?
> A. Yes, for everyone who believeth not is condemned and everyone
> who believes is justified.
> Q. 3. But must not repentance and works meet for repentance go
> before faith?
> A. Without doubt, if by repentance you mean conviction of sin,
> and by works meet for repentance, obeying God as far as we can,
> forgiving our brother, leaving off from evil, doing good and using
> his ordinances according to the power we have received.[8]

This last answer sounds as though you are supposed to act like a believer before you are one. Such actions predate justifying faith, but they
are made possible by the presence of God's prevenient grace. Prevenient
grace makes possible a pre-justified expression of faith he spoke of as
"the faith of a servant." Calvin and Luther would fold repentance and
justification into one great transaction. Wesley, seeking to follow what
he perceived in scripture, saw repentance as a distinct, preparatory step.
In "On Working Out Our Salvation," he writes:

> But what are the steps which the Scripture directs us to take, in the
> working out of our own salvation? The prophet Isaiah gives us a
> general answer touching the first steps which we are to take: "Cease
> to do evil; learn to do well." If ever you desire that God should work
> in you that faith where of cometh both present and eternal salva-
> tion, by the grace already given, fly from all sin as from the face of a
> serpent; carefully avoid every evil word and work; yea, abstain from
> all appearance of evil.[9]

Wesley goes on to list an array of righteous behaviors that could easily be described as post-justification actions. Following on he raises the obvious question as to how such works could be possible for the unsaved. His answer we have already seen in describing prevenient grace: "There is no man that is in a state of mere nature; there is no man, unless he has quenched the Spirit, that is wholly void of the grace of God...of what is vulgarly called 'natural conscience.' But this is not natural; it is more properly termed 'prevenient grace.'"[10]

In the 1744 Minutes we read of a result of this grace that helps explain why "works meet for repentance," while not *good* in the sense of able to save or expressing the presence of Christ in a believer are nonetheless of value. Wesley says that "repentance is *a low species of faith*" (emphasis mine).[11]

Prevenient grace helps us to get up on the porch of the house of religion to begin the journey of faith. There, God's Spirit stirs as our hearts are prepared to walk into the house through the door of sincere trust in what God in Christ has done. This "low species of faith" characteristic of repentance, to borrow an expression Wesley employed in "The Scripture Way of Salvation," is "only *remotely* necessary."[12] But this pre-justification "faith" is of genuine worth. Although no comparison is complete, repentance is akin to the premarital engagement period. Certainly there is love at work during that often exciting time of preparation. However, in the normal course of events there must come a time of yielding and commitment in order for love to find its truest and most transforming expression.

Repentance: A Time for Training Wheels

For quite some time I was rather flummoxed by Wesley's teaching that repentance was necessary before believing. Understanding that repentance is a low species of faith made possible by prevenient grace, but not the same as justifying faith, explains Wesley's meaning. This low species of faith and the works meet for repentance, thus clarified as manifestations of grace, are consistent with Wesley's overall view of grace, works, and faith.

In the early days of the revival, Wesley began to display his gifts of administration in the rise of the United Societies. These assemblies were divided into classes and bands, forerunners of "small groups" through which so much disciple-making has taken place in recent times. Woven into the DNA of these spiritual formation groups were the Rules of the United Societies. I confess paying little attention to these guidelines until serving as a district superintendent under Bishop B. Michael Watson, who frequently referenced these rules. In 2007 the rules were given a much wider audience with the publication of Bishop Reuben Job's *Three Simple Rules—A Wesleyan Way of Living*. The simplest statement of the rules as Wesley wrote them is as follows: (1) do no harm, (2) do good, and (3) attend upon all the ordinances of God (public worship attendance, public scripture exposition/reading, receiving the Lord's Supper, private prayer, searching the scriptures privately and fasting).[13]

Repentance is a low species of faith made possible by prevenient grace, but not the same as justifying faith.

Bishop Job's presentation of the rules was a contemporary interpretation. He rephrased the third rule with these words: "stay in love with God." In addition to the "ordinances" listed above Wesley actually had a very clear menu of examples under the first two rules, the origin of which can be found in his early discipline of persons desiring to participate in the life of the new Societies. Richard Heitzenrater notes that in February 1743, Wesley traveled to Newcastle where he found the young society lax in its discipline of participants. Before he was finished, sixty-four persons (of approximately nine hundred) were expelled from the society. The list of their offenses included:

- two for cursing and swearing;
- two for habitual Sabbath-breaking;
- seventeen for drunkenness;
- two for retailing spirituous liquors;
- three for quarrelling and brawling;
- one for beating his wife;
- three for habitual, willful lying;
- four for railing and evil-speaking;
- one for idleness and laziness; and
- twenty-nine for lightness and carelessness.[14]

Two days later, Wesley wrote *The Nature, Design, and General Rules of the United Societies.* In order to *join* a Society, persons were required to demonstrate only one condition: "a desire to flee from the wrath to come, to be saved from their sins."[15] Those who wished to *remain* involved in the Societies, however, were expected to keep the three rules. Interestingly enough, the rules as he fleshed them out bore a striking resemblance to the reasons why people had been expelled from the Newcastle society. The list of ordinances is a precise enumeration of the kinds of means of grace that "quietist" Moravians (an example of the passive practitioners of Christianity that Wesley opposed) would have people omit. Wesley knew, Heitzenrater notes, the now-printed rules would disturb some of the members of the society, yet he examined the classes a second time with the rules in hand. Charles Wesley was apparently an even tougher examiner than John, in some instances culling out "counterfeits and slackers" among those who had passed John's inspection.[16]

It could be misleading to speak of the rules as "a Wesleyan way of living." Wesley himself was clear in saying a person could keep the rules perfectly and still be a stranger to the religion of the heart, as he would identify true Christianity. This is likely why Bishop Job, in giving the rules a contemporary spin, modified the third rule to include love of God as its central characteristic. There is no doubt timeless wisdom in the rules that applies to believers throughout the journey of faith.

However, their original design appears to be as aids to the process of repentance. As possible, "works meet for repentance," the rules are heavy-duty spiritual-formation *training wheels*, external supports intended to keep seekers upright until, by the Spirit's presence engaging the fully trusting heart, the believer finds an intuitive balance within. They can also serve in the life of a justified person engaging in what was called "evangelical repentance," or continued transformation.

Wesley scholar Ken Collins observes that in using the rules to guide the societies, Wesley was demonstrating that "the very design and purpose of the Methodist societies was one of repentance, of preparing sinners to 'flee from the wrath to come.'" He continues, "On the one hand there is vigorous human activity as the newly repentant ones obey God; on the other hand, this obedience and labor is ever preceded and empowered by the convincing grace of God, 'according to the measure of grace which we have received.'"[17] Similar to the laws of God, the rules of the societies had no power to save. But they could provide occasions for encounters with the Holy Spirit.

Repentance: The Wake-Up Call

An elementary-age daughter came to her pastor father with a theological question. She clearly recalled her father talking about hearing from God. She then declared, with real disappointment, that *she* never heard from God. Her father thought a moment and then said, "Do you remember recently when you told me about another girl in your class who didn't have a friend and something told you that you should be her friend?" "Yes." Her father paused and in just a moment his little girl declared, "Oh! So that's him!" Carrying out the intent of rule number two, "do good," had led to a grace-filled epiphany.

Repentance is the process of awakening and responding to God, though we may often not recognize the origin of the awareness growing within us. Wesley's rules were a method of enabling seekers to put themselves in situations where both their failings and God's goodness could awaken an ever clearer sense of need for mercy and the possibilities of grace.

Repentance is the process of awakening and responding to God, though we may often not recognize the origin of the awareness growing within us.

Standing on the porch of repentance seeking admission into the house will usually find the seeker trying a variety of keys. The low species of faith that motivates this effort takes the seeker into the heart of Hebrews 11:6, "It's impossible to please God without faith because the one who draws near to God must believe that he exists and that he rewards people who try to find him." Repentance grows out of a limited faith that God does exist. It continues forward with the hope that the behaviors "meet for repentance" will somehow receive God's reward. Ultimately, however, the thought of earning a pass mark and hence God's approval must be surrendered. What is left is grace. Yet, Wesley would never forget this is *cooperant* grace that graciously enables us to participate in the process.

Our search for God was only possible because God long ago preveniently initiated the search for us. Christian author Ken Gire tells the story of a little girl who lived on the edge of a forest. The forest was her second home. But one day she ventured too far and realized she was lost. The ebbing light of the day brought with it worries, both for her and her now searching parents. They called her name but got no answer. So their search grew more intense.

The little girl tried this and that path to no avail. Branches lashed her face and tears ran down her cheeks. Finally at the end of her energies she curled up on a big rock and fell asleep.

With passing hours friends and neighbors joined in the search, eventually discouraged by the darkness of the night, but not the girl's father. He searched through the night and into the dawning hours. At last he saw his daughter asleep on the rock. Running with all his might he began calling out her name. The noise awakened the girl with a start. She rubbed her eyes. And reaching out to him, she caught his embrace.

"Daddy," she exclaimed, "I found you!"[18]

Wake up! The Lord is waiting to find you!

Questions for Discussion

1. What did we learn about the grace of God in the last chapter that makes legal repentance (changed behavior before justification) possible?

2. In what ways do we wake up in the process of repentance?

3. What did Wesley mean by "works meet for repentance"? (see Minutes of 1744 Annual Conference)

4. How does the engagement period prior to marriage reflect the nature of repentance before justification?

5. What is the connection between repentance and "a desire to flee from the wrath to come, to be saved from sins"?

6. In what way(s) could the three rules of the Methodist societies be spoken of as training wheels?

7. Have you had any experience such as C. S. Lewis describes?

8. How do you now see that God was seeking you long before you sought God?

Belief #6

Justification: Humble Faith Receives Pardon

Our experiences of repentance on the porch of the house of religion will be as unique as we are. Even so, the gracious purpose of the porch is to bring us to the gateway of justification. Jesus artfully yet powerfully illustrates the struggle and the blessing of repentance in three parables recorded in Luke 15. In the first two, the parables of the lost sheep and the lost coin, Jesus directly states that there is incomparable joy in God's presence over the repentance of even one sinner. The third parable, a story of a father and his sons, is a masterpiece of simplicity and clarity, illustrating the power of repentance to open the door to reconciliation and rebirth.

As the search is undertaken for the lost sheep and the lost coin, we observe prevenient, gracious energy at work to restore that which is lost and helpless to achieve self-restoration. The third story is a tale of personal relationships, revealing humankind's disconnection from its heavenly Father and the universal need for redemption. One of Wesley's understandings of the workings of grace that may sound illogical is illustrated by this story: repentance precedes faith.

Both sons exhibit spiritual blindness to their father's heart of grace and love. The younger son, like Adam and Eve, acted to gain control and ended up losing it. The elder brother took a passive-aggressive tack, playing the role of the good son while inwardly estranged from his father. The pivot point in the parable occurs when the younger brother begins to experience the kind of new awareness of self and of the father characterizing repentance. Trudging back home, rehearsing words of confession, his "change of mind" encourages faith, not in himself but in his father.

It is illuminating to observe the lack of change of mind in the elder brother. Although still physically near his father, he fails to see either himself or his father in a new light. Absent such repentance there is a corresponding absence of faith. Adopting the role of victim, virtually always a toxic attitude, he completely misses the significance of the father's saving, restoring grace. The younger brother *woke up* and *gave up* on any hope of self-rescue. He rejected self-pity. The elder brother, though assured by his father of continued inclusion in the father's resources, remained asleep, failing to connect with his father's gracious character.

The story ends with the younger brother receiving signs of his father's saving grace, the best robe and the ring for his finger. At the same time he is born again to his father, as the father declares, restored to all of the possibilities of sonship. Meanwhile, the elder brother who never physically left home exhibits his deadness to the father's heart by shunning the celebration of his brother's new life. In him there is no repentance, and there is no faith. Until the elder brother finds his way to the porch of repentance and wakes up, there will be no new life for him.

Justification (and All Progress in Grace) Begins with What God Does

C. S. Lewis, participating in a conference in Britain on comparative religions, walked into a room where participants were discussing the question of Christianity's unique contribution to world religion. He asked, "What's the rumpus about?" Upon learning of the question at hand he quickly replied, "Oh, that's easy. It's grace."[1]

My answer would have been "Jesus." But Lewis's general intuition was valid. Through Jesus Christ God has taken a unique, divine initiative to restore us, providing prevenient, convincing, justifying and sanctifying grace. The practical questions then center around: how does God's grace engage us and we it? Those were the questions at the core of several of the controversies surrounding John Wesley.

Let's begin by recalling the words of Hebrews 10:19-24:

> Therefore, brothers, since we have confidence to enter the Most Holy Place by the blood of Jesus, by a new and living way opened for us through the curtain, that is his body, and since we have a great priest over the house of God, let us draw near to God with a sincere heart in full assurance of faith, having our hearts sprinkled to cleanse us from a guilty conscience, and having our bodies washed with pure water. Let us hold unswervingly to the hope we profess, for he who promised is faithful. And let us consider how we may spur one another on toward love and good deeds.

In Jesus Christ a new and living doorway has been opened through which we may draw near to the holy God. By grace our hearts (one of Wesley's orienting concerns) can relate to God with freedom. Believers' baptism, universally understood as a time of witness, is essentially an occasion for pointing to God as the source of grace, the one who opens the door to new life. This "outward and visible sign of an inward and spiritual grace" is a way of believers declaring, "Look what God in Christ has done! I believe it! I receive it! He who has promised is faithful. This sacrament is a symbol of what God is doing in my heart."

Hebrews 10:24 reminds us of Wesley's other orienting concern, responsible grace. Love and good deeds are central to how grace impacts a believer's life to enable cooperation with God. Wesley stirred many a "rumpus" over his determination to affirm experiential internal religion (heart) as well as grace-enabled outward response-ability (deeds).

We Experience a Change in Status and a Change in Self by Grace

Terms that take center stage in this controversy regarding grace are *imputed* and *imparted*:

- to impute is essentially a legal expression meaning "credit to" another person
- to impart, when referring to grace, means to move beyond legal attribution to actual transference of qualities of spirit/character from one party to another; this is not a change of status—it is a direct reception of a quality of life.

Wesley spoke of these distinctions by differentiating between what God does *for* us and what God does *in* us. His sermon "The New Birth" begins with these words: "If any doctrines within the whole compass of Christianity may be properly termed fundamental they are doubtless these two—the doctrine of justification, and that of the new birth: the former relating to that great work which God does *for us*, in forgiving sins; the latter to the great work which God does *in us*, in renewing our fallen nature."[2]

Wesley was again conjunctive in the sense that he proclaimed both a legal change in the believers' relationship with God and an actual ongoing change in the lives of those who come to Jesus in faith.

Imputed Grace Makes Possible Our Justification

Wesley understood that imputed grace, while not exhaustive in capturing the full scope of God's new and living way of salvation, was essential in accomplishing the making of disciples. Imparted grace deals with the *power* of sin in a believer's life. Imputed grace addresses the *guilt* of sin in a believer's life. This takes us to the meaning of justification.

Believe it or not, Wesley's understanding of justification is not complicated. In his sermon "Justification by Faith," he writes, "The plain scriptural notion of justification is pardon, the forgiveness of sins."[3] At the first Annual Conference, Monday, June 25, 1744, about seven o'clock in the evening, the *Minutes* record, "We began to consider the doctrine of Justification....Q. 1. What is it to be justified? A. To be pardoned and received into God's favor and into such a state that, if we continue therein, we shall be finally saved."[4]

As the revival began Wesley's single favorite text in the first half-year was 1 Corinthians 1:30, a passage that affirms imputed grace: "It is because of God that you are in Christ Jesus. He became wisdom from God for us. This means that he made us righteous and holy, and he delivered us." From the beginning to the end of salvation there will be no place for trusting in our own virtue. Faith in the merits of Jesus Christ, his righteousness and holiness, will forever remain the firm foundation of all who claim salvation.

In Charles Wesley's journal entry for Friday, February 24, 1738, we read of his ongoing conversation with the Moravian Peter Bohler. Bohler came to the place of asking him, "Do you hope to be saved?" Charles answered, "Yes." "For what reason do you hope it?" Bohler continued. Charles replied, "Because I have used my best endeavors to serve God." Charles continues his record of the conversation, "He [Bohler] shook his head, and said no more. I thought him very uncharitable, saying in my heart, "What, are not my endeavors a sufficient ground of hope? Would he rob me of my endeavors? I have nothing else to trust to."[5] Awakening to the freedom by faith to trust in grace and not their endeavors was the major turning point in both Charles's and John's lives. Wesley labored to help others come to this turning point and grasp the crucial nature of salvation by grace through faith.

Another related battle was the fight against abusing grace by using it as a crutch rather than a gift with which the believer is enabled to cooperate with God. Wesley's response to this misuse of imputed grace is seen in his sermon "The Lord Our Righteousness."

> There is no true faith, that is, justifying faith, which hath not the righteousness of Christ for its object.... In the meantime what we are afraid of is this: lest any should use the phrase, "the righteousness of Christ," or, "the righteousness of Christ is 'imputed to me,'" as a cover for his unrighteousness. We have known this done a thousand times. A man has been reproved, suppose, for drunkenness. "Oh, said he, I pretend no righteousness of *my own*: Christ is *my righteousness*." Another has been told that "the extortioner, the unjust, shall not inherit the kingdom of God." He replies with all assurance, "I am unjust in myself, but I have a spotless righteousness in Christ." And thus though a man be as far from the practice as from the tempers of a Christian, though he neither has the mind which was in Christ nor in any respect walks as he walked, yet he has armour of proof against all conviction in what he calls the "righteousness of Christ."[6]

Wesley scholar Stephen Gunter describes this sermon, "The Lord Our Righteousness," as "Wesley's theological attempt to preserve the concept of a sovereign God who graciously saves sinners, without forfeiting his emphasis on human integrity and responsibility."[7] In actuality that would describe much of Wesley's ministry in the later decades of his life.

Justification is something done for us and we receive it as a gracious gift by faith alone (sola fide).

Wesley's strong emphasis on what is now termed responsible grace did not mean a rejection of imputed righteousness. The merits of Jesus Christ are, in Wesley's own words, our only hope. Justification is something done *for* us and we receive it as a gracious gift by faith alone (*sola fide*). To attempt flight with only one wing, Wesley was firmly convinced, is to end up in a circle of either passive, possibly sin-excusing "faith," or, on the other hand, works righteousness. Wesley saw the former as the more frequent danger but understood the necessity of both workings of grace in seeking to live out a biblical faith.

The Workings of Grace: Put Away the Cookie Cutter

If grace is both imputed and imparted, it is logical that its impact could be both instantaneous and gradual. The receiving of justification is so entirely the work of God that the moment may or may not be memorable. What matters is the eventual realization that by grace through faith we have received pardon. In a letter to Mary Cooke in 1785 Wesley makes it clear the nature of the experience in itself is not what matters:

> There is an irreconcilable variability in the operations of the Holy Spirit on (human) souls, more especially as to the manner of justification. Many find him rushing in upon them like a torrent, while they experience "The o'erwhelming power of saving grace." ... But in others he works in a very different way: "He deigns his influence to infuse; Sweet, refreshing, as the silent dews." It has pleased him to work the latter way in you from the beginning; and it is not improbable he will continue (as he has begun) to work in a gentle and almost insensible manner. Let him take his own way: He is wiser than you; he will do things well.[8]

What this letter is actually addressing is the workings of prevenient grace and its experiential results in justification. At some point in time by faith we must claim for ourselves the truth of 1 John 1:9, "But if we confess our sins, he is faithful and just to forgive us our sins and cleanse us from everything we've done wrong." To believe this is to be justified by grace through faith. Wesley would not make this a hitching post. Justification was declared to be a signpost, pointing forward to a greater deliverance and fruitfulness.

I can say without fear of exaggeration that my personal journey in coming to terms with justifying grace has not been cut and dried. In my early years of faith I heard great evangelical preaching about grace while in college and learned the history of grace in multiple seminary classes. As a United Methodist pastor, I often held grace as central in my teaching and preaching. Even so I was far from done in comprehending and being comprehended by grace.

My first full-time church was the Victory Memorial United Methodist Church in the southeast part of inner-city Indianapolis. Our parsonage had five locks on the back door. Children could never be left alone outside. Victory Memorial was a congregation of 150 members, a third of whom were homebound. Most of the active members no longer lived in the neighborhood.

Given the poverty all around us, there were many requests for assistance, telephone calls from all over the city, and people knocking on our door daily. One of those seeking help became a significant part of my life. Russell H. appeared our first summer along with his wife and little girl. His daughter was about one year old, like our daughter. Both girls were adorned with golden curls. Across the months and years ahead it would become easy to say no to Russell, but thoughts of that little girl would always give me pause.

I got an education in the welfare system working with Russell. He was somewhat slow mentally and usually made what money he could by washing cars on the numerous used car lots along Washington Street to the north of where we lived. Their little family stayed in the kinds of places where you pay rent by the week in advance. They moved often. The last Christmas we served in Indianapolis I arranged to bring Russell and his family to the church Christmas party. Victory Memorial was a blue-collar church whose people were salt-of-the-earth Hoosiers with a gift for good fellowship. When I pulled up to the house where Russell and his family were living, I could see the external stairs leading up to their room. It was a cold December day and I had on a heavy corduroy coat. I blew my horn and Russell appeared in the door at the top of the stairs. He had on a short-sleeved Hawaiian-print shirt. I knew it was the best shirt he owned.

In the early spring of the next year, the day before Palm Sunday, I was busy working on my sermon. Like all preachers I was eager for it to be good, hoping the special Sunday would coax less-active people back to worship. The telephone rang. It was Russell. They were being kicked out of the place where they had been living. He had no money. The only place they could go was to Russell's mother's house in the southern part of the city. I knew them well enough to understand that to be only a short-term fix, but it was the only remedy. He asked if I could take them to his mother's.

It would be difficult to exaggerate how much I did NOT want to do that, for any number of reasons. But... it seemed they had no other option, so I left my uncompleted sermon on the desk and went to find them. They were living in one room in a large old house. When I knocked on the door I was greeted by someone who appeared to be a member of the Hell's Angels, complete with a heavy beard and black leather clothing. The crowd inside that house was not folks you would take home to mama.

I made my way upstairs where Russell, his daughter, and his once-again pregnant wife had been staying. On the floor of the room was a mattress that looked like someone had used it under their truck while changing oil. The only furniture was a chest of drawers with the legs on one side missing, causing it to sit at a stark angle on the floor. All of their possessions were in two large garbage bags. Russell took one and I took the other, making our way through the "angels."

Russell sat in the front seat of the car and his wife and little girl sat in the back. There was not much to say. I had spent many hours on the telephone with Russell during nights when it was too dangerous to go visiting. Besides, my mind was whirling with thoughts of that sermon for Palm Sunday. At some point along the way my mind fell silent and then from within I "heard" a voice. It was not externally audible but in my mind it was clear and quite unlike any usual thought. Immediately I sensed it was the voice of Jesus. This is what he said to me: *Don, in your relationship to me…you are Russell.* The spiritual formation of young pastors is often provided by those who ask no tuition but unconditional love.

Immediately my absolute dependence on the grace of God was as clear as a bright summer morning. It was the holy love of God that motivated the giving of God's only Son for the fallen world of which I was a part. There was no merit in me. That was many years ago and nothing I have learned or experienced since has changed what I came to see with much greater clarity that day. Imputed grace necessarily opens the door of justification through which we walk by faith.

Justification: What God Does for Us and Begins in Us

Famous German theologian and martyr Dietrich Bonhoeffer made the term "cheap grace" a theological household term. John Wesley was way ahead of him. Justification, Wesley understood, is not a destination. Wesley scholar Colin Williams reflects Wesley's view:

> Justification is the real basis and beginning of the Christian life. It is an 'objective' work in the sense that it arises not from a change in us but from a word of God to us—"Son, thy sins be forgiven thee." But when the word is heard, something happens in us. For faith is the opening of the life to Christ. It is new birth. Then sanctification follows because of Christ's presence.[9]

Justification is pardon. God is beginning something significant in us by doing something for us we are helpless to do for ourselves.

Justification is pardon, opening the prison doors of sin and death offering a new beginning for the heart and soul.

Justification is pardon, introducing the orphan to a new family initiating a renewed identity as a child of God and the opportunity to conform to the image of the one Jesus taught us to call Father.

Justification is pardon, satisfing the holy God who calls all who trust in Jesus Christ for salvation. It is an invitation to seek loving holiness without which no person shall comprehend their potential as a creature made in the image of that holy God.

Justification is pardon, sparking a new beginning, releasing God's power to "take up your cross *daily.*" God is beginning something significant *in* us by doing something *for* us we are helpless to do for ourselves.

Wimps Need Not Apply!

This challenge from chapter 1 does not mean we are saved by courage or effort. It implies we should understand that salvation, while an utter gift, is also a calling, an enlistment in a great army empowered by heart-transforming grace.

The three key doctrines on which this study is built—repentance, faith, and holiness—were, as noted by Wesley scholar Ted Campbell, "distinctively Methodist" as opposed to what would comprise a broader listing of evangelical doctrines. They focus on the journey from helplessness to healthiness, from the stirrings of faith to the maturity of faith working through love. Campbell notes that this can be seen in the structure of a variety of Methodist hymnals going back to the time of the Wesleys themselves.

Clapper, noting this distinct clustering of doctrines in Wesleyan ministry, seeks to clarify the relationship of means and ends in Wesley's development and deployment of theology. What was *foundational* or the ultimate concern for Wesley, he declares, was not proper academic doctrine. These doctrines form the core of Wesley's thinking, as Clapper puts it, "because they are *most important for the foundational formation of disciples*, because they are *indispensably formative of the heart* is most likely the reason they *became* distinctively Methodist." Wesley, centuries before Stephen Covey's *Seven Habits of Highly Effective People*, began with the end in mind (habit #2).[10]

The "end" of Christ's coming was the glory of God revealed in redeemed and renewed human lives. Jesus did not come so we could pass a systematic theology class. "It's good that you believe that God is one. Ha! Even the demons believe this, and they tremble with fear" (James 2:19). In *A Plain Account of Genuine Christianity* Wesley declares, "A man may assent to three or three-and-twenty creeds; he may assent to all the Old and New Testament (at least as he understands them) and yet have no Christian faith at all."[11] To that end, the grace of God must not only minister pardon but also be "formative of the heart" and facilitate transformation. Justification is a doorway, *the* doorway into the house where the image of God is renewed in us and we go on to perfection. On to *what?* Fret not. Grace will remain the key in the rest of the journey of faith.

Questions for Discussion

1. What is the difference between imputed grace and imparted grace?

2. Why did Wesley resist an exclusive focus on imputed grace?

3. What can we learn about repentance from the two brothers of the Prodigal Son story?

4. Do you remember a specific moment of being justified/born again by grace through faith? If not, how did you come to the realization of being forgiven and/or reborn?

5. What did "In your relationship with me you are Russell" mean? Does it mean anything to you?

6. Explain what it means to say, "Justification is not a destination."

B e l i e f # 7

Initial Sanctification: We Find Our Identity in God's Family

Since the bicentennial year of Methodism, 1984, I have been presenting monologues as John Wesley. It has given me a unique opportunity to move beyond the facts of his life. For a number of years, for example, I wrestled with the importance of his heartwarming experience at Aldersgate Street. Why did he almost never mention it again in his vast writings? Did that experience of assurance deserve the place of prominence history has given it? I found myself pondering the possibility that going outside the walls of the church to preach was the most important moment of his life. Had he not, as he put it, "submitted to be more vile," and in obedience stepped out of his comfort zone into new ministry, all the Aldersgate experiences in the world might have made no difference.

Upon further reflection I now see that the warmed heart of Aldersgate and the obedient act of field preaching are another example of the conjunctive work of God's grace. Remembering Wesley's orienting concerns, it was not a fluke that Wesley used the word *heart* in describing what happened at Aldersgate Street. Neither was it a fluke that this change of heart lead to a radical new engagement with co-operant grace, leading to new fruitfulness. The "warming" of Wesley's heart by justifying grace, his new sense of being "inside" the house of sanctification, released the Holy Spirit to bear the gifts of love, joy, and peace in ways Wesley had never known.

Being Justified Releases a New Motive

From 1725 when Wesley entered into a serious pursuit of God's will until his experience at Aldersgate in 1738, we observe an unrelenting search for certainty of his salvation. In 1735 his father, Samuel, died. His father's final words were, "The inward witness, son, the inward witness, that is the proof, the strongest proof of Christianity."[1]

The next year, at the conclusion of a terrifying trip to Georgia inwardly seeking what he described as his own salvation, on Saturday, February 7, Wesley is greeted in Savannah by Moravian theologian August Spangenburg. Here is Wesley's record of that encounter:

> He told me he could say nothing till he had asked me two or three questions. "Do you know yourself? Have you the witness within yourself? Does the Spirit of God bear witness with your spirit that you are a child of God?" I was surprised, and knew not what to answer. He observed it, and asked, "Do you know Jesus Christ?" I paused, and said, "I know He is the Savior of the world." "True," replied he; "but do you know He has saved you?" I answered, "I hope He has died to save me." He only added, "Do you know yourself?" I said, "I do." But I fear they were vain words.[2]

After two more years of travail, continuing to battle an unabated disease regarding his salvation, he finally entered into a perceptible, though hardly "enthusiastic," awareness of forgiveness. The most famous words from his journal, May 24, 1738, record this crossroads.

> In the evening I went very unwillingly to a society in Aldersgate-Street, where one was reading Luther's preface to the epistle to the Romans. About a quarter before nine, while he was describing the

change which God works in the heart through faith in Christ, I felt my heart strangely warmed. I felt I did trust in Christ, Christ alone for my salvation: And an assurance was given me, that he had taken away *my* sins, even *mine*, and saved *me* from the law of sin and death.[3]

I recall hearing a sermon about Wesley in which the preacher said the most important thing in Wesley's journey to faith was the modifiers. There was a time, the preacher proclaimed, when Wesley knew of *a* Savior. Then it became clear to him that Jesus was *the* Savior. Finally at Aldersgate Wesley could say, "Jesus is *my* Savior." That is a rather informal way of saying it, but it reflects Wesley's journey from prevenient to convincing to justifying (and initially sanctifying) grace. It was a journey from fear to love as the chief motive of his life.

Would It Matter to You if You Lived in the Slave Quarters or in Your Father's House?

Two expressions that are part of the Wesleyan lexicon of scriptural Christianity are "the faith of a servant" and "the faith of a son."[4] Using the image of the house of religion, the faith of a servant is generally the life of a person on the porch, the seeker. The faith of a son or daughter is the changed relationship represented by living in the Father's house. It does not require theological sophistication to grasp the great difference between being the Father's slave and being the Father's child. Listen to Wesley's words in his sermon "The Discoveries of Faith," preached late in his life (1788):

> The faith of a servant implies a divine evidence of the *invisible* and the *eternal* world; yes, and an evidence of the *spiritual world*, so far as it can exist without living experience. Whoever has attained this, the faith of a servant, "feareth God and escheweth evil"; or, as it [emphasis mine] is expressed by St. Peter, "feareth God and worketh righteousness." In consequence of which he is in *a degree*

(as the Apostle observes), "accepted with him."...Nevertheless, he should be exhorted not to stop there; not to rest till he attains the adoption of sons; till he obeys out of love, which is the privilege of all the *children* of God.[5]

"He obeys out of love." Wesley went to Georgia out of fear. Several years later, back in England, he went into the open fields out of love. After Aldersgate it would take Wesley a number of months to work through confusion created in his mind by Moravian teachings that understood justification to produce immediately mature holiness. Once he did, living in the faith of a son empowered Wesley into a ministry truly far more than he could have asked or thought (Eph 3:20).

Wesley's "Ask" (the Point Where the Salesperson Calls for a Response): Believe/Receive

"Offer them Christ." This was Wesley's way of focusing his lay preacher's message. It was an elementary call to trust Christ for pardon. But Wesley knew that offering Christ included several major possibilities:

- the faith of a servant—influenced by prevenient and convincing grace, one who fears God and works righteousness (Acts 10:35), who is *thus far acceptable* in the sense of being a sincere seeker moving toward redemption
- justification—pardon for disobedience to God's will
- new birth—an inner renewal of the heart and quickening of God's image (prolific spiritual life author Ken Boa says that "renewing us in God's image" is God's "purpose statement")[6]
- adoption into the family of God as a consequence of justification and new birth
- the witness of the Spirit that we are children of God—the faith of a child of God

- the work of sanctifying grace to purify our motives and develop in us "the mind that was in Christ Jesus" (to keep us growing in grace)

All of this was wrapped up in the directive "offer them Christ." It could include all of the graces of God. We know that "offering Christ" was usually an expression pointing to repentance and justification. Wesley might have said, "Let people know that in Jesus Christ God can change the pronouns they use to talk about the Savior." Wesley's favorite book was 1 John and he often used the following portion to offer Christ to his hearers: "This is the message that we have heard from him and announce to you: 'God is light and there is no darkness in him at all.'...If we claim, 'We don't have any sin,' we deceive ourselves and the truth is not in us. But if we confess our sins, he is faithful and just to forgive us our sins and cleanse us from everything we've done wrong" (1 John 1:5, 8-9).

If John Wesley was standing beside you as you read this he might well ask, "Do *you* believe this? Have *you*, by faith, accepted this great and precious promise?" In 1787, in a letter to Theophilus Lesser, Wesley emphasized the need for such a personal appropriation of God's mercy in Jesus Christ: "To believe the being and attributes of God is the faith of an heathen. To believe the Old Testament and trust in Him that was to come was the faith of a Jew. To believe Christ gave himself *for me* is the faith of a Christian" (emphasis mine).[7] For those unsure of their salvation he was still calling the baptized and unbaptized alike to expect the blessing of forgiveness and new birth, and to expect to know in their hearts that reconciliation with God has taken place. This "knowing" was spoken of as "the witness of the Spirit" and/or "the assurance of pardon." Engaging the gift of pardon is the beginning of a new process of transformation through sanctifying grace. Moving from justifying to sanctifying grace, believers can understand this change as being adopted into God's family.

*Engaging the gift of pardon
is the beginning of a new process
of transformation through
sanctifying grace.*

The Remarkable Joy of the Fact of Our Adoption into God's Family

The paradigm of adoption as a metaphor of justification/new birth/ initial sanctification is not a major distinct doctrine in Wesley's theology. However, identification as a *son*, *daughter*, or *child* of God, as in "the faith of a son," is woven through his teaching. Experiencing "the spirit of adoption" is a common phrase associated with persons he would describe as *real* Christians.

Adoption as a picture of a grace-restored relationship was employed by the Apostle Paul (Rom 8:15, 23; Gal 4:5; Eph 1:5). When a child is adopted that person is in a real sense born again, given a new identity, a new community, new resources, and a new inheritance. What makes the concept of adoption so powerful is the dynamics of love and grace that potentially raise this change of relationship above a legal covenant.

Maddox quotes from *An Earnest Appeal to Men or Reason and Religion* in speaking of Wesley's understanding of adoption:

> To enjoy faith is to receive the Spirit of Adoption. Accordingly, "adoption" is one of Wesley's designations for restored participation in God. It is the initiation of Christianity's central goal: "Restoring the due relations between God and (humanity), by uniting for ever the tender Father and the grateful, obedient (child)." The importance of this is that our grateful perception of our reconciling Father is precisely what invites and empowers us to be obedient children.[8]

As a novice pastor the first book of the Bible I attempted to preach through was Galatians. It was during that study I first began to grasp the blessed concept of adoption as a picture of redemption. Years later I became acquainted with the story of the DeBolt family. Their amazing journey has been told in a book, *19 Steps Up the Mountain,* and in an Academy Award–winning documentary, *Who Are the DeBolts? And Where Did They Get 19 Kids?* What makes the DeBolts' story so powerful is the makeup of their family. Six of the children were biological. The rest, eventually fourteen others (one was added after the documentary was made) were adopted. As remarkable as that would have been, the most striking feature of the family becomes clear when you meet them. They included:

- Tich and Anh, war-wounded, paraplegic children from Vietnam;
- Sunee, a girl from Korea, paralyzed due to polio;
- Karen, an African American child, congenital quadruple amputee (congenital amputee is a term sometimes used to mean congenital absence);
- Wendy, Korean, blind, suffering from abuse; and
- John ("J.R."), a Caucasion, paraplegic, blind child with spina bifida.

The grace extended to all of these children manifested itself, in terms of this study, in both responsible grace and heart-changing grace. The title of their story, *19 Steps Up the Mountain,* refers to the circular staircase in the DeBolt house. It was a literal mountain to children whose appendages didn't support them (or didn't exist), or who simply could not see. That great obstacle became an opportunity for grace to lead to victory as handicapped children helped other handicapped children learn to live in the real world.

Again and again in the DeBolt story you observe these children being motivated to move beyond fear. In the knowledge that "nothing could separate them" from the security of parental love, that love helped them "cast out fear."

One day Tich overheard Dorothy pray out loud. He comments that she seems to talk with God all the time and then asks if she will do him a favor.

"Sure. What?"

"You ask Him make me walk again, Ma?"

Dorothy was so moved by the request she began crying and ran out of the room. Tich followed her, wanting to offer comfort. She assured him that his brain, as well as Anh's (the other Vietnamese paraplegic child) brain, would carry them further than her legs had carried her.

He replied, "Listen, Ma, the next time you talk to God, you tell Him it's OK to take brains back and give me legs." They laughed.

From an adjacent room Anh overheard the laughter and came to see what had prompted it.

"Tich wants God to take his brains and give him back his legs."

"God make deal like that?"

"I don't think so."

Anh's face sobered. "Maybe God already give us deal. We in this family, ain't we?"[9]

If the holy, tough, unalterable adopting love of Christ grips the heart, then all things are possible.

There is no way to understand Wesley's great expectations for Christian living if your mind is still in the legal state, under law and not grace. But if the holy, tough, unalterable adopting love of Christ grips the heart, then all things are possible. This change of relationship is one of the facts of being in Christ. But more than a fact, it ushers us into a new world of relationships that can change our lives.

We Can Experience the Deep Joy of an Assurance of Pardon

Wesley believed that regeneration/new birth brought to life spiritual senses by which the adopted child of God sensed an inner connection with their Creator/Redeemer. This affirmation of "perceptible religion" was profoundly crucial to Wesley's understanding of the Christian life. In one of his letters to "John Smith" he declares, "No man can be a true Christian without such an inspiration of the Holy Ghost as fills his heart with peace and joy and love, which he who perceives not has it not. This is the point for which alone I contend; and this I take to be the very foundation of Christianity."[10]

For Wesley perceptible religious experience meant a sense of personal reconciliation and connection with God's mercy. "You didn't receive a spirit of slavery to lead you back again into fear, but you received a Spirit that shows you are adopted as his children. With this Spirit, we cry, 'Abba, Father.' The same Spirit agrees with our spirit, that we are God's children" (Rom 8:15-16). Wesley's understanding and proclamation of assurance, while always a part of his gospel proclamation, would undergo some tweaking.

In the early years of itinerant preaching Wesley bound justification and assurance together, two sides of the same coin. The message was: you can't have one without the other. The *Minutes* of the first Annual Conference, June 1744, are often quoted in this regard. "All true Christians have such a faith as implies an assurance of God's love...that no man can be justified and not know it....Q. 6. But may not a man go to heaven without it? A. It doth not appear from Holy Writ that a man who hears the gospel can."[11]

At the next Annual Conference this was modified to allow for persons who claimed justification by faith but had not experienced an inner assurance of pardon. These were spoken of as "exempt cases." That could have described Wesley before Aldersgate. With such allowances made, calling for people to expect an inner witness of the Spirit was the norm. While Wesley coveted this experience for all believers, it was the joy of a perceptible awareness of being in fellowship with God through Jesus Christ that Wesley desired for all Christians. These words from his sermon "The Almost Christian" describe his goal for believers:

> May we all thus experience what it is to be not almost only, but altogether Christians! Being justified freely by his grace, through the redemption that is in Jesus, knowing we have peace with God through Jesus Christ, rejoicing in hope of the glory of God, and having the love of God shed abroad in our hearts by the Holy Ghost given unto us.[12]

Wesley saw assurance of pardon and inclusion in the family of God as scriptural. His personal experience of assurance was clearly long sought and a major crossroads in his own spiritual journey. But with the passing decades of the revival he came to see that he had likely done some harm with his strong call to expect assurance. Wesley's sermon, "On Faith" (1788) is an autobiographical retelling of the evolution of his thinking about the necessity and place of assurance. As he remembers it, in the early days of the revival he and his fellow Methodist preachers did not yet understand the relationship between what he would come to speak of as the faith of a servant and the faith of a child of God. Another way of putting this would be to say they had not yet understood the way in which God's grace lead people from early levels of faith to the next. The faith of a servant, an early stage of belief primarily based on fear of God, was not an appropriate stopping place in the journey of faith. However, in time he came to see it was acceptable to God as the beginning of wisdom under the influence of prevenient grace.

Usually persons in this faith of a servant stage, when asked if they knew their sins were forgiven, would, Wesley reports, reply they did not. In the absence of assurance of pardon, Wesley and his preachers would respond with the declaration that those lacking such assurance were still under condemnation. This, Wesley would come to see, was "apt to make sad the hearts of those God had not made sad."[13]

As their understanding of growth in faith matured, rather than discouraging those not yet experiencing assurance, Wesley and the Methodist preachers would advise, "Hitherto you are only a *servant*; you are not a *child* of God. You have great reason to praise God that he has called you to his honorable service. Fear not. Continue crying unto him: 'and you shall see greater things than these.' . . . There is no reason why you should be satisfied with the faith of a materialist, a heathen, or a deist; nor with that of a servant."[14]

Even in this correction there remains an unwillingness to marginalize the place of assurance and the faith of a son/child of God that it enables.

Ever a reasonable man, Wesley also came to see another reason why an absolute insistence on inner assurance was not logical. "That some consciousness of our being in favour with God is joined with the Christian faith I cannot doubt; but it is not the essence of it. A *consciousness of pardon cannot be the condition of pardon*" (emphasis mine).[15] So, Wesley never ceased to call seekers to expect, by faith, the inner witness of the Holy Spirit confirming their adoption into the family of God. At the same time, like works of piety or mercy, he understood assurance to be not a necessary condition of salvation but the normal consequence of the presence of God in Christian believers.

Assurance is not a necessary condition of salvation but the normal consequence of the presence of God in Christian believers.

One of the most interesting facts about Wesley and assurance is this: he virtually never, that we know of, used his own sense of assurance as proof of the Christian faith or as a tool of witness. If the Aldersgate experience had not been recorded in his journal, we might never have taken note of it. The basis of his witness was scripture, not experience.

The Renewed Heart: A Wesleyan Way of Life

Although no ritual or mechanical model was taught by which new birth should be secured, Wesley consistently identified its nature. He proclaims:

> From hence it manifestly appears what is the nature of the new birth. It is that great change which God works in the soul when he brings it into life: when he raises it from the death of sin to the life of righteousness. It is the change wrought in the whole soul by the almighty Spirit of God when it is "created anew in Christ Jesus," when it is "renewed after the image of God," in righteousness and true holiness.[16]

One of the motivations for writing this study was a deep concern that as persons interested in a vital faith became acquainted with Wesley's rules for the societies, they might think the rules an adequate description of "a Wesleyan way of life." Wesley himself made it clear numerous times that following the rules could result in a dead faith apart from the transforming work of the Spirit. A typical example of Wesley's warnings is found in his sermon "A Blow at the Root or Christ Stabbed in the House of His Friends." He begins by affirming the satisfaction many felt in observing the three rules: "by doing no harm, doing good, going to the church and sacrament. And many thousands sit down content with this, believing they are in the high road to heaven." He continues:

> Yet many cannot rest here.... They well know, that although none can be a real Christian, without carefully abstaining from all evil, using every means of grace at every opportunity, and doing all possible good to men; yet a man may go thus far, may do all this, and

be but an Heathen still. They know this religion is superficial; it is but as it were skin-deep. Therefore, it is not Christianity; for that lies in the heart; it is worshiping God in spirit and in truth; it is no other than "the kingdom of God within us."[17]

Wesley was clear all through his years of ministry that neither orthodox beliefs nor orthodox behaviors were the essence of Christian faith. Yes, they were *necessary* but not in the same way that grace received by faith is *necessary*. A "Wesleyan way of life" will always spring forth from what God does in the heart to enable things like doing no harm, doing good, and observing the spiritual disciplines to be done in the strength of holy love.

My ninety-two-year-old retired United Methodist pastor father-in-law is in the latter stages of dementia. His talking has diminished and he requires help with everything. One day my wife was in the room talking with some of the staff at the United Methodist retirement facility where her parents live. Her dad was not participating and the conversation was kept low in an effort to discretely discuss his issues. Suddenly he began singing:

Blessed be the name.
Blessed be the name.
Blessed be the name of the Lord.
Blessed be the name.
Blessed be the name.
Blessed be the name of the Lord.

The verse that followed seemed especially poignant for a person in his condition:

I never shall forget that day,
Blessed be the name of the Lord,
When Jesus washed my sins away,
Blessed be the name of the Lord.[18]

93

This was the default testimony of a life lived in the joy of an assurance of pardon and the adoption of sonship. The mind was feeble but the heart was alive. Truly such is a Wesleyan way of life.

The assurance of pardon, a dimension of Christian experience which Wesley greatly valued, was more than a satisfying feeling. It was an organic aspect of the blossoming of justification into initial sanctification. Being restored in the image of God, adopted into the family of God, was an immersion into grace intended to reorient all things in those who were becoming new creatures in Christ.

Questions for Discussion

1. Why are the three rules of Methodist Societies (Do no harm, Do good, Observe the ordinances of the church) not adequate to identify the Christian faith or "a Wesleyan way of living"?

2. "To believe Christ gave himself for me is the faith of a Christian." Do you believe this? What change has this belief made in your life?

3. Does having a religious experience mean becoming an extremist? Why or why not?

4. What place does assurance have in your life?

5. What does the statement "a consciousness of pardon cannot be the condition of pardon" mean?

6. Adoption is a form of new birth. How does this idea help us see being born again with fresh eyes?

B e l i e f # 8

Holy Love: Discipleship Combines Heart and Life

John Wesley believed the only way to be truly happy was to be holy. No, that wasn't any more politically correct in his day than in ours. Filmmaker Woody Allen comes closer to contemporary sensibilities, describing religion as "guilt with holidays." This from the man who quipped, "Not only is there no God, but try getting a plumber on the weekends."[1] Watercooler conversation does not include chat about sanctification. Such work-a-day world exchanges often exemplify C. S. Lewis's observation: "It would seem that Our Lord finds our desires, not too strong, but too weak. We are half-hearted creatures, fooling about with drink and sex and ambition when infinite joy is offered us, like an ignorant child who wants to go on making mud pies in a slum because he cannot imagine what is meant by the offer of a holiday at the sea."

Holiness? Wimps need not apply. Sanctifying grace is high-powered medicine that holds the promise of the truest healing and deepest satisfaction.

One of Wesley's favorite succinct descriptions of sanctification was: the mind of Christ in us. This is based on the Philippians 2 passage that described Jesus's self-emptying, cross bearing obedience. The mind of Christ is a way of seeing life, God, and self in a totally new way. Thus radical language is used in speaking of this transformation:

- We lose our lives.
- We are crucified with Christ.
- We count ourselves dead to sin.
- All things become new.

Philip Yancey captured the irony of sanctifying grace when he described Jesus's call, "Take up your cross and follow me," as "the least manipulative invitation that has ever been given."[2]

Hopefully you are aware of where you are personally in relation to Wesley's house of religion—near the porch, on the porch, through the door, or in the house. Too, it should be ever clearer that the grace of God is what makes progress possible, renewing our hearts and enabling us to be response-able. Spiritual formation authority Dallas Willard makes this important distinction about Christian growth:

> It is not a project of "life enhancement," where the "life" in question is the usual life of "normal" human beings—that is, life apart from God. It is, rather, the process of developing a different kind of life, the life of God himself, sustained by God as a new reality in those who have confidence that Jesus is the anointed One, the Son of God. "Believing in him we have life in his name" (John 20:31, PAR). Those "in Christ"—that is, caught up in his life, in what he is doing, by the inward gift of birth from above—"are of a new making (*ktisis*). The 'old stuff' no longer matters. It is the new that counts" (2 Corinthians 5:17, PAR). Here in this new creation is the radical goodness that alone can thoroughly renovate the heart.[3]

In this same vein, again, Yancey writes that we must come to a place of understanding ourselves as sinners "who cannot please God by any method of self-improvement or self-enlargement. Only then can I turn to God for outside help–for grace–and to my amazement I learn that a holy God already loves me despite my defects."[4]

Wesley relentlessly declared that the scriptures offer much more hope for grace-enabled transformation in this life.

Far from being forgiven and then left to do the best we can until death, Wesley relentlessly declared that the scriptures offer much more hope for grace-enabled transformation in this life. In "The Great Privilege of Those That Are Born of God," he describes the change brought into a believer's life by the new birth/regeneration: "a vast inward change; a change wrought in the soul by the operation of the Holy Ghost, a change in the whole manner of our existence."[5] Bible translator J. B. Phillips also affirms the centrality of God's gracious action in the regeneration of human life when he writes, "We may...point out the great difference that has come to exist between the Christianity of the early days and that of today. To us it has become a performance, a keeping of rules, while to the people of the early days it was an invasion of their lives by a new quality of life altogether."[6]

We see this "invasion" dramatically in the disciples' lives in the early chapters of Acts. When Peter and John appear before the Jewish court in Acts 4 it is noted that they were unschooled (no rabbinical training). "The council was caught by surprise by the confidence with which Peter and John spoke. After all, they understood that these apostles were uneducated and inexperienced. They also recognized that they had been followers of Jesus" (Acts 4:13). Did you hear that? The Sanhedrin, themselves extremely well-schooled, time-toughened rabbis who had only contempt for Jesus, were *astonished*! What they would have no way of comprehending was that the Spirit of Jesus had invaded Peter's and John's lives.

Jesus Is Our Yokefellow

Wesley's high view of the new birth/regeneration/initial sanctification/full sanctification rests on the New Testament proclamation of Christ in us/us in Christ. In Ephesians 3:17, 19, the Apostle Paul prays a soaring prayer for believers centered in the desire "that Christ will live in your hearts through faith," and the longing that those who walk with

Jesus "will be filled entirely with the fullness of God." Those later words for Wesley point to the possibilities of Christlikeness, in his words, "A perfection far beyond a bare freedom from sin."[7] As Paul writes, "It is because of God that you are in Christ Jesus. He became wisdom from God for us. This means that he made us righteous and holy, and he delivered us. This is consistent with what was written: *The one who brags should brag in the Lord!*" (1 Cor 1:30-31). Trust in the Lord who is *in* your heart and in the hearts of fellow believers, we are told, and don't expect to carry the yoke of sanctification alone.

Holiness Is Always Centered in Scripturally Informed, Grace-Empowered Holy Love

For many years, to me, sanctification essentially meant living above sin. I kept a subconscious score sheet of good and not good behaviors. My spiritual life was motivated by pride. For the most part, what I was reading of John Wesley's writings appeared to support this understanding of sin-avoidance as the chief priority of living a Christian life. Wesley says a lot about "not sinning" and clearly favored 1 John, especially verses such as, "Every person who remains in relationship to him does not sin. Any person who sins has not seen him or known him" (1 John 3:6).

Consider these words from the conclusion of Wesley's sermon "The End of Christ's Coming":

> Be not content with any religion which does not imply the destruction of the works of the devil, that is, of all sin. We know weakness of understanding, and a thousand infirmities, will remain while this corruptible body remains. But sin need not remain: this is that work of the devil, eminently so called, which the Son of God was manifested to destroy in this present life. He is able, he is willing, to destroy it now in all that believe in him. Only be not straitened

in your own bowels! Do not distrust his power or his love! Put his promise to the proof! He hath spoken: and is he not ready likewise to perform? Only "come boldly to the throne of grace," trusting in his mere mercy: and you shall find, "He saveth to the uttermost all those that come to God through him!"[8]

For a time I took shelter in interpreting 1 John's strong statements as saying Christians do not sin *habitually*. But no, Wesley would have none of that. In his sermon "Christian Perfection," he references 1 John 3:8-9, "He that committeth sin is of the devil....Whosoever is born of God does not commit sin; for his seed remaineth in him, and he cannot sin, because he is born of God." Wesley then comments, "Indeed it is said that this means only, he sinneth not *wilfully*; or he doth not commit sin *habitually*; or, *not as other men do*; or, *not as he did before*. But by whom is this said? By St. John? No. There is no such word in the text, nor in the whole chapter, nor in all this Epistle, nor in any part of his writings whatsoever."[9]

There is no rounding off corners by Wesley. He was true to scripture as it spoke plainly to him.

Holiness is more than living above sin.

Overcoming willful, *intentional* sin as a result of the new birth/initial sanctification was an important hallmark of Wesley's scriptural expectations for Christians. Sin *remained* but did not *reign*. It could be controlled through the grace of new birth, regeneration of the heart and ongoing abiding in Christ. Further, he affirmed the possibility of *entire* sanctification, a state of grace in which inner rebellion against God, the *being* of sin, was subdued. As essential as these interpretations of scripture were to his overall ministry, his understanding of scripture pointed to an even higher goal of holy living, as quoted above, "A perfection far beyond a bare freedom from sin." That perfection was the more excellent way of holy love as the standard for those who follow Jesus Christ. I was beginning to understand that holiness is more than living above sin.

It Was the Worst of Times

Wesley understood that the great majority of those to whom he preached were far from ready to internalize that message. So he devoted significant energy to calling people to repentance, including believers who needed to take seriously the possibility that the sin remaining in them did not have to reign.

Like all of us, Wesley was a person of his time, and it was a time when morality was in eclipse. This infected every level and segment of society, including the clergy. During my seminary years I visited England and experienced one of those divine serendipities that give a foretaste of heaven. It also put me more in touch with Wesley's England.

In Camberly, we made the acquaintance of Captain Godfrey Buxton, member of a family that had sent pioneer missionaries to both Africa and Japan. Conversing with Captain Buxton was, for me, like spending time with the Apostle Paul. When we parted company he gave me a copy of *England: Before and After Wesley* by J. Wesley Bready, which his brother Alfred had given to him as a Christmas gift in 1938.

This book made a case for the opinion that the Wesleyan revival in England had been a watershed in Anglo-Saxon history, providentially influencing both England and the United States with spiritual and moral leaven. Contemporary historian Henry Rack suggests that Bready overreaches in the credit he assigns to Wesley.[10] Such criticism aside, *England: Before and After Wesley* paints an unimpeachable picture of eighteenth-century England as profoundly coarse in its entertainments, shallow in its spirituality, carnal in its morality, and cruel in its justice. Child labor was common. Children along with adults were subject to hanging for minor offenses. The slave trade became a major economic engine. In mid-century, the "Gin Age" reached its peak, with eleven million gallons of gin consumed. Sports like bear, bull, and badger baiting, cock fighting, boxing (including women), gambling (lotteries raised money for projects such as the British Museum), and prostitution were additional exhibits of a morally foundering society. Bready begins the book with these words: "In 1738, the year of Wesley's 'conversion,' Bishop Berkeley in his *Discourse Addressed to Magistrates and Men in Authority*, declared that morality and religion in Britain had collapsed 'To a degree that has never been known in any Christian country....Our prospect,' he averred, 'is very terrible and the symptoms grow worse from day to day.'"[11]

Looking back from the next century, William M. Thackery, author of *Vanity Fair*, portrayed the court life of King George II (1727–1760) in these dramatic words:

> No wonder the clergy were corrupt and indifferent amidst this indifference and corruption. No wonder that the sceptics multiplied and morals degenerated so far as they depended on the influence of such a King. No wonder that Whitefield cried out in the wilderness, that Wesley quitted the insulted temple to pray on the hillside. I look with reverence on those men at that time. Which is the sublimer spectacle—the good John Wesley surrounded by his congregation of miners at the pit's mouth, or the Queen's chaplains, mumbling through their morning office in the ante-room, under the picture of the great Venus, with the door opened into the adjoining chamber, where the Queen is dressing, talking scandal...or uttering sneers...? I say I am scared as I look around at this society—at this King, at these courtiers, at these bishops—at this flaunting vice and levity. Whereabouts in this court is the honest man? Where is the pure person one may like?[12]

Karl Mennenger's 1973 book *Whatever Became of Sin?* would have had a different spin in the eighteenth century, but the inference of the title could have applied to significant segments of English society. In twenty-first-century England, the word *sin* itself has been removed from the *Oxford Junior Dictionary* along with other church-related terms with the rationalization that, like agrarian terms that no longer fit urban life, it had fallen out of use in a secular culture.

Wesley Called 'Em Like He Believed Scripture Saw 'Em

It should come as no surprise that Wesley's longest writing dealt with what one scholar termed "a perennially unpopular topic"—original sin.[13] Enlightenment rationalism, anti-evangelical deism, upper-class permissiveness, resistance to Christian piety remaining from the aftertaste of Cromwell's reign, and sermons generally classified by one historian as "dull, duller, and dullest" were some of the causes and effects inoculating against sensitivity to righteousness.[14] In "Scriptural Christianity" (1744), Wesley blasts his Oxford peers as "a generation of *triflers; triflers with God, with one another, and with your own souls.*"[15]

Forty-six years later, as both his life and the eighteenth century were waning, matters among the intelligentsia were no better. In his sermon "The Deceitfulness of the Human Heart" (1790), Wesley directly addresses what Outler describes as "the Enlightenment's mortal threat to historic Christianity" because of its "new and bold affirmations of human autonomy."[16] No wonder Wesley preferred common people who, though sinners by nature, were at least further removed from the corruption of "society."

In scripture Wesley saw a high calling, great expectations if you will, for the potential of human lives redeemed and invaded by God's Spirit. Carnal English culture did not create his theology of sin and redemption, but it did impact his priorities in bringing the gospel to bear on his world. As a gifted and practical evangelist he was especially constrained to contend for "plain old scriptural Christianity" that presented a high calling and promised power over willful disobedience to God.

Wesley's Vision: Not Just against Sin, but for Holy Love

In his consideration of church ministry, *Center Church*, pastor and author Tim Keller writes of the crucial importance of "theological vision" in doing ministry. Wesley's scriptural Christianity was central to his remarkable vision of the power of:

- field preaching (mass media);
- gatherings of the Methodist societies (worship beyond traditional forms);
- scripture framed in poetry set to tunes of the day (contemporary music);
- medical clinics and prison ministry, and so on (outreach orientation);
- sacrificial stewardship (generosity); and
- attending to corporate and personal connection to the usual means of grace (spiritual disciplines/formation).

Had Wesley just been "against" sin, the righteousness that accompanied the revival might have not "exceeded that of the scribes and the Pharisees." It is important to understand that living above willful sin was not what Wesley saw in scripture as "the main thing."

James Fowler in his study of adult development and Christian faith, *Becoming Adult, Becoming Christian*, makes this strategic observation: "The most revealing aspect of any theory of human development is the character of the last stages."[17] The latter stages of grace as Wesley taught them were matters of the "mind of Christ" ruling in the heart and life. The goal was not sinlessness, though obedience should follow from seeking the goal and holiness ought to accompany the fullness of God in a human life. The highest pursuit and longing was God's holy, single-minded, "perfect" love as the standard and motive of life. Scripturally, this is a no-brainer in light of the greatest commandments being to love God with one's total being and one's neighbor as oneself. Similarly the

Apostle Paul makes a remarkably categorical declaration in Galatians 5:6, "The only thing that counts is faith expressing itself through love."[18]

Sanctification is holy love: a single-minded spirit of servanthood and unflinching obedience to the Father, not out of fear of rejection or judgment, but driven by grateful faith, humble trust, and abiding love.

Jesus had not come to promote the righteousness of the scribes and the Pharisees. "I say to you that unless your righteousness is greater than the righteousness of the legal experts and the Pharisees, you will never enter the kingdom of heaven" (Matt 5:20). Jesus taught and modeled "perfection far beyond bare freedom from sin," as Wesley identified it, a manner of life captured in the voluntary taking up of the cross. It is a single-minded spirit of servanthood and unflinching obedience to the Father, not out of fear of rejection or judgment, but driven by grateful faith, humble trust, and abiding love.

How Much Room Is There for Sin If You Are Full of God?

Thoughts of sinlessness as the ultimate goal fall short of human potential as creatures made in God's image. Wesley's chosen successor as superintendent of the Methodist societies, John Fletcher, said, "It seems to me but a small thing to be saved from all sin. I want to be filled with all the fullness of God."[19] A focus on behavior tends toward a constant introspection, which feeds a distorted self-love and easily turns Christian faith into another treadmill of attempted self-salvation/sanctification. Again, Fletcher writes, "The work of sanctification is hindered...by holding out the being *delivered from sin* as the mark to be aimed at, instead of being *rooted in Christ*, and *filled with the fulness of God*, and *with power from on high*."[20] This brings to mind E. Stanley Jones's observation that the holiness movement would have been better off had it focused less on holiness and more on Christ who makes people holy.

In his essay "The Weight of Glory," C. S. Lewis begins by observing, "If you asked twenty good men to-day what they thought the highest of the virtues, nineteen of them would reply, Unselfishness. But if you asked almost any of the great Christians of old he would have replied, Love. You see what has happened? A negative term has been substituted for a positive."[21]

For Wesley, the greater goal was God's grace restoring the image of God in a human life.

This same dynamic goes into action when avoiding sin is seen as the high-water mark of Christian holiness. For Wesley, the greater goal was God's grace restoring the image of God in a human life. Sounding much like Fletcher, Wesley says that real religion is "a restoration of man . . . not only to the favour, but likewise to the image of God; implying not barely deliverance from sin but the being filled with the fullness of God. . . . Everything else, whether negative or external, is utterly wide of the mark."[22]

Holy Love Is the Bull's-Eye

Wesley's first university sermon (1730) was entitled "The Image of God" on the text Genesis 1:27, "So God created man in his own image."[23] In another early sermon (1734) Wesley preached on Luke 10:42 where Jesus speaks of the "one thing" that was needful. This one thing is identified by Wesley as "the renewal of our fallen nature."[24] The renewal of the heart as an orienting concern finds its origin here. And the "real nature" of "true religion," Wesley would affirm, lies "in 'the hidden man of the heart.'"[25] He concludes "The Circumcision of the Heart" with this injunction:

> "Set your heart firm on him, and on other things only as they are in and from him." "Let your soul be filled with so entire a love of him that you may love nothing but for his sake." "Have a pure intention of heart, a steadfast regard to his glory in all your actions." "Fix your eye upon the blessed hope of your calling, and make all things of the world minister unto it." For then, and not until then, is that "mind in us which was also in Christ Jesus," when in every motion of our heart, in every word of our tongue, in every work of our hands, we "pursue nothing but in relation to him, and in subordination to his pleasure"; when we, too, neither think, or speak, nor act, to fulfil our "own will, but the will of him that sent us"; when whether we "eat or drink, or whatever we do, we do all to the glory of God."[26]

It is not difficult to find Wesley's own words written in support of the primacy of holy love in a believer's life. One of the most pointed would have to be in his sermon "On Perfection" in which he proclaims:

> What is then the perfection of which man is capable while he dwells in a corruptible body? It is the complying with that kind command, "My son, give me thy heart." It is the "loving the Lord his God with all his heart, and with all his soul, and with all his mind." This is the sum of Christian perfection: it is all comprised in that one word, love. The first branch of it is the love of God: and as he that loves God loves his brother also, it is inseparably connected with the second, "Thou shalt love thy neighbor as thyself." Thou shalt love every man as thy own soul, as Christ loved us. On these two commandments hang all the law and the prophets: these contain the whole of Christian perfection.[27]

In the sermon "On Zeal" Wesley describes the priorities of the faith in a way bringing to mind a target of six concentric rings. The outermost ring is *the church*. Next are *works of piety*. Moving inward toward the center we find *means of grace, works of mercy, holy tempers,* and the bull's-eye, *love*: "*love* sits upon the throne, which is erected in the inmost soul; namely, love of God and man, which fills the whole heart, and reigns without a rival."[28] In identifying the qualities of an *altogether* as opposed to *almost* Christian, he says, "whosoever has this faith, thus 'working by love,' is not *almost* only, but *altogether* a Christian."[29]

The true target: the abiding, holy love of God seen with clarity in Jesus and shed abroad in our hearts by the Holy Spirit.

To understand this does not answer all the questions of discipleship. But it at least gets us aiming for the true target: the abiding, holy love of God seen with clarity in Jesus and shed abroad in our hearts by the Holy Spirit.

Questions for Discussion

1. What did J. B. Phillips mean by saying that in the early days of the Christian movement Christianity was "an invasion of their lives by a new quality of life altogether"?

2. What do you think it means to be "filled with all the fullness of God"?

3. Some interpreters of 1 John suggest that the author meant we do not sin *habitually* if we are Christian. Why did Wesley reject this interpretation?

4. Clearly Wesley was born into a low period in Christian morality. What might this say about the spiritual possibilities in the twenty-first century?

5. How would you interpret Galatians 5:6: "But faith working through love does matter"?

Belief #9

We Are Better Together: Christianity Is a Social Faith

During the height of the Civil War, Abraham Lincoln often took refuge at a Presbyterian church in Washington, DC. He sat off to the side to avoid notice. Following the loss of his own son, he again found his way to the church in the company of an aide. After the service, the aide inquired as to the president's opinion of the sermon. Lincoln replied, "I thought the sermon was carefully thought through, eloquently delivered."

The aide said, "You thought it was a great sermon?"

Hat in hand Lincoln answered, "No, I thought he failed."

"He failed? Well, how? Why?"

"Because he did not ask of us something great."[1]

Wesley refused to be guilty of such a failure. In his *Notes* on the New Testament related to 2 Corinthians 13:11, "Be perfect" (KJV), he wrote simply, "Aspire to the highest degree of holiness."[2] C. S. Lewis put it in mid-twentieth-century language: "The command 'Be ye perfect' is not idealistic gas. Nor is it a command to do the impossible. He is going to make us into creatures that can obey that command."[3] Wesley wholeheartedly agreed.

Something Great? How about the Great Commandment?

Jesus does not ask of us something great, to borrow Lincoln's term. Jesus *commands* us to do something great. In Matthew 22:37-39 we find the record of Jesus's "Great Commandment," to love the Lord our God with all of our hearts and souls and minds, and our neighbors as ourselves. Whatever else you may decide about Wesley and holiness, keep one thing straight: Wesley did not invent "the highest degree of holiness." It was not an obsessive-compulsive personality or a neurotic perfectionistic temperament that put holiness on the front burner of Wesley's message. Wesley clearly heard Jesus command something great, and no matter how persecuted or misunderstood he was, he would not abandon the high calling. If you do not like holiness, take it up with Jesus, not John Wesley. In the next chapter holiness terms such as "entire sanctification" and "Christian perfection" are addressed in the hope that clarity regarding these very Wesleyan terms will help interpret what Jesus and the scriptures are calling disciples to do and be.

Sanctification is seeking the mind of Christ, a relationship with God of obedience and fruitfulness.

The discovery that the heart of holiness is holy love rather than avoiding sin was huge in my understanding "plain old scriptural Christianity." Surprise! Plain old scriptural Christianity is not essentially justification. In his classic study of Christian discipleship, *The Divine Conspiracy*, Dallas Willard includes a chapter entitled "Gospels of Sin Management." These are ways of interpreting the Christian faith as a method of being forgiven and heading for heaven. Yes, being forgiven is huge. Walking off the porch of God-discovery and self-discovery, then turning toward God through the door of justification by grace through faith in Jesus Christ, is an awesome transition. But the point of it all remains to be pursued. Wesley would call this main point having the image of God restored in us. As noted before, one of his favorite succinct definitions of sanctification is seeking the mind of Christ, a relationship with God of obedience and fruitfulness. The end result is a life of holy love. I almost always preface the word *love* with the adjective *holy*, pointing to love as the scriptures define it as opposed to the one-size-fits-all cheap grace that masquerades for love in the postmodern world. Holy love brings us to the subject of this chapter: community.

Before looking at the Methodist tradition regarding community, in the spirit of John Wesley, let's be reasonable. What is the greatest commandment and its partner? Jesus clearly proclaimed loving God and neighbor and self were the Creator's highest priorities. God, as revealed in scripture, is a community: Father, Son, and Holy Spirit. Our neighbor is part of the community in which we live. Our self, as affirmed by English poet John Donne who was the dean of St. Paul's in London early in Wesley's life, is not an island. If the greatest commandment is eminently tied to community, wouldn't it make sense that our spiritual formation would likewise be best undertaken in the company of others?

The Importance of Community

God's image in humankind included people thriving in relationships of mutual trust and dependency. The Trinity is the archetype of such relationships. Very early on the Creator affirms this with the well-known declaration, "It's not good that the human is alone" (Gen 2:18). Sin in human nature creates a kind of centrifugal force that inhibits community. Before they were deemed unsafe, riding a merry-go-round on a playground was an exhilarating experience. For those who didn't hold on tight, the power of centrifugal force became obvious. A careless rider was thrown away from the center with no small amount of force. Reading the early chapters of Genesis offers a look at how a corresponding kind of force in human nature became universal following the first act of sin. Cain and Abel, Noah and his neighbors, and the Tower of Babel are primitive case studies of this centrifugal energy at work.

Sin in human nature creates a kind of centrifugal force that inhibits community.

Human pride, a diabolical combination of self-worship and self-hate, fuels this force within. Prevenient grace helps the natural person awaken to the existence of this inner power and its unavoidable consequences. Repentance marks the beginning—and growth—of a desire to embrace God's ways. Justification brings pardon for sin. Initial sanctification initiates the restoration, the regeneration, of the image of God and the expelling of the "earthly, sensual, devilish" mind.[4] Entire sanctification is full control by the mind of Christ that has displaced the centrifugal force of sin as the ruling power within. The kingdom of God is within us, beginning in a new heart. It is not designed to mature in isolation. The greatest commandments being to love, by default, require relationships in which they are lived out.

Clarifying "Social" Christianity

Wesley understood and repeatedly elevated a principle that can easily be lost in the common language of evangelical Christianity and misinterpreted in the lexicon of progressive Christianity. That is the importance of what he termed "social Christianity." In "Upon Our Lord's Sermon on the Mount, IV," Wesley devotes much of the message to explaining his understanding of this principle. There are two common misunderstandings of what he had in mind. The first is this: social religion, it is said, refers to what today is spoken of as "social action." Wes-

112

ley has plenty to say about an active faith. But this is not the case in his endorsement of "social religion." "When I say this is essentially a social religion," Wesley says in clarification, "I mean not only that it cannot subsist so well, but that it cannot subsist at all without society, without living and conversing with other men."[5] In other words, Christianity virtually demands community (unless you are alone on a deserted isle). "Christianity is essentially a social religion, and ... to turn it into a solitary religion is indeed to destroy it."[6] In the mature years of the revival he wrote, "Those who will not meet in class cannot stay with us."[7]

This final quote refers to the class meetings that became so important to the continuation of the revival and the maturing of believers. Meeting in "societies" to support or participate in spiritual causes was commonplace in England. Wesley scholar Richard Heitzenrater displays a chart in his study of Wesley and Methodism illustrating the existence of religious societies more than fifty years before the Wesleyan evolution of such tools of spiritual formation.[8] Around the turn of the eighteenth century, the Society for Promoting Christian Knowledge was founded. It became a model and source of support for local societies. John Wesley was a corresponding member of the SPCK. Later it would be the Society for the Propagation of the Gospel that would send John and Charles to Georgia.

Early Methodism: A Community Made Up of Communities

At Oxford and in Georgia little societies were part of Methodism's embryonic beginnings. Wesley referred to these as the first and second "rise" of Methodism. In 1738 a society at Fetter Lane in London, a Moravian group from which Wesley would later part company, was a major evolution of this paradigm for the development of the revival. He identified this as the third rise of Methodism, indicating the significance of community to the awakening.

The focus would soon shift to the Foundry Society in London and to rapidly growing societies in Bristol, where Wesley witnessed the sort of moving of the Spirit described in Jonathan Edward's awakening in New England.[9] The larger societies were places of instruction, exhortation, and support. In those societies there were small groups called "bands" made up of five to ten people who banded together for intentional spiritual support. The membership of each band was homogeneous with groups organized by gender and marital status. Maximum honesty and openness was the goal. Heitzenrater observes:

> Wesley's rules for the band societies were a modification of the Fetter Lane Society rules; they had more specificity in the questions asked of band members as to their state, sins, and temptations. The point was to encourage faith working through love, that the love of God might be shed abroad in their hearts and lives. To this end, the bands met regularly (at least once a week) for intense spiritual intercourse.[10]

These groups soon came under the general identification of "United Societies" as the Methodist connection developed. In Bristol, early 1742, larger societies were divided into "classes," neighborhood subdivisions of about a dozen people. Each class had an assigned leader. This organization was created as a fund-raising apparatus. The leaders were responsible for raising twelve pence a week toward debt retirement on the New Room, a building constructed to house the growing societies. If the weekly offering fell short of the goal, the leaders agreed to make up the difference.

As leaders made their weekly rounds to collect from class members they discovered problems: family disputes, drunkenness, and other less-than-holy behavior. Wesley quickly recognized the pastoral opportunities in this organization. The leaders, with whom Wesley would meet weekly when possible, became spiritual overseers. Eventually, the classes began to gather together, organized geographically. As this evolution continued, the classes became incubators for justifying grace with the three General Rules as the *training wheels* for those desiring to flee the wrath to come and work out their salvation. To his credit, John Wesley (and Charles as well) did not allow this structure to degenerate into a social club. Discipline was closely enforced and those who were careless in their lives were put into "penitent" bands or rejected from participation altogether until evidence of true repentance was shown.

Community/accountability was the "secret" for the longevity of the Wesleyan revival.

The result was a decades-long continuation of the spirit of revival and the maturation of believers in holy love. Accountability, instruction, and support were means of grace as Wesley insisted upon and carefully administered "social" Christianity. George Whitefield, who was by far the superior preacher, rued his own lack of such administrative wisdom, speaking of those under his ministry as "a rope of sand."[11] Community/accountability was the "secret" for the longevity of the Wesleyan revival.

Writing of faith development, James Fowler makes this observation: "Communities play a critical role in this process by providing relational contexts where we are known personally (over time), where we are taken seriously, and where we are invited to submit our images of ourselves and our vocations to trusted others, who are informed by the community's 'script' and core story, for correction and/or confirmation."[12]

At my ordination service, the speaker spoke of other people as "sandpaper in the hands of God" to be part of "finishing" his servants. In "Upon Our Lord's Sermon on the Mount, Discourse IV," Wesley says much the same thing declaring that meekness, which he calls an essential Christian trait, "cannot possibly have a being, it has no place under heaven, without an intercourse with other men. So that to attempt turning this into a solitary virtue is to destroy it from the face of the earth."[13] Christianity without intentional human interaction is a destructive oxymoron. So community was an essential part of the DNA of Methodism from its beginnings.

Conjunctive Spiritual Formation: Heart and Community

It must be noted as a second possible misunderstanding that Wesley's unrelenting emphasis on social religion was not a rejection of personal religious experience. The religion of the heart was an orienting principle of Wesley's theology. In 1778 Wesley records a visit to Oxford during which he mused, "What lovely mansions are these! What is wanting to make the inhabitants of them happy? That without which no rational creature can be happy—the experimental knowledge of God."[14] It was not personal interior faith and experience that Wesley rejected. It was "solitary" religion. Again in "Discourse IV," Wesley declares, "Christianity is essentially a social religion, and...to turn it into a solitary religion is indeed to destroy it."[15]

There should, in reality, be no need to affirm the importance of community in the Christian life. Children should not have to be reminded that they are part of a family. If such consciousness is lacking, it ordinarily means something is wrong. As Wesley proclaimed the gospel, it was clearly personal but not private, in part interior but not individualistic. What does this have to do with community? Consider the following, thoughtfully.

When Jesus spoke about the vine and branch relationship, he was clearly identifying the need for each person to be attached to him. This is a personal relationship. In that relationship the individual receives life-giving grace and truth that enables repentance, pardon, and personal growth in grace into the mind of Christ. But this is not a private relationship. Jesus did not say that he would plant a vine in every heart so each individual could have their own independent relationship and power supply. Some might interpret the Holy Spirit in the believer in that way, yet when did the Spirit come? On the day of Pentecost when the disciples were in one accord, in ultimate community. Following Pentecost, did everybody run off in their own direction? No, it was just the opposite. As an expression of the remarkable union created in the Spirit's outpouring, they held things in common.

When Jesus taught the pattern prayer, the pronouns referring to those praying are all plural. In John 17 in his prayer for all believers Jesus prays for unity (vv. 20-23). The picture of a bottle filled with salt water floating in the ocean has been used to describe the meaning of Christ in us and us in Christ. This does not eliminate unique individuality. It rejects solitary individualism.

When the prodigal son returned home, he was offered symbols of union with his father and family, a ring and robe. He had tried individualistic methods, ended up with the pigs, and came home to share in the grace of his father's house. That was personal salvation, life-changing and heart-changing spiritual formation. There is great irony here. Had the son remained independent in his heart, he would have remained dead to his father. His spirit of repentance did not earn mercy, but it opened the door for mercy to enter a humbled heart and begin a "great change," as Wesley referred to the new birth.[16] The new heart would be fundamental to his new life and continue as a game changer for the rest of his days. Even so, that new life was not an independent, autonomous life. It had made possible a new orientation to life and to his father.

In 1 John we are told, "The one who has the Son has life" (5:12). Earlier in the letter we are also told that believers "have an anointing from the holy one" (2:20). Such statements can sound individualistic. However, at the conclusion of the section dealing with the anointing, John strongly directs his readers to "remain in relationship to him" (2:27). We are not isolated "holy units." We are in Christ, together.

Christ in Us—Us in Christ

Noted evangelical New Testament scholar Ben Witherington wrote a study of this paradigm, *A Shared Christian Life*. Writing as one who "grew up...in the shadow of Billy Graham's home," his understanding of salvation was clarified as he listened to the New Testament. He writes,

> The New Testament says absolutely nothing about individuals having a "personal" relationship with Jesus, in that precise sort of language, especially if by "personal" one means private or individualistic apart from anyone else's relationship with Christ.... [To] "ask Jesus into my life [is] (yet another phrase nowhere to be found in the New Testament)" [bracketed words are mine].

Such statements are probably stunning to many readers. He goes on to explain his concern:

> What is wrong with [this picture] is that *while it is true that God in Christ becomes central and thus a vital part of a Christian's life after conversion, what primarily happens at conversion is not Christ becoming a part of "you" or being absorbed by "you" but quite the reverse—you become a part of Christ's body: you become "in Christ." The dominant language in Paul's letters about this matter refers to persons who are "in Christ." In fact the phrase "in Christ" is the Pauline equivalent for "Christian"—he does not use the term "Christian" to refer to converted individuals!* [emphasis in original][17]

Christian spiritual formation is broken and incomplete apart from the interaction of believers with one another and the world in the spirit of holy mutuality and love.

In their study of predestination and related subjects, British authors Roger Forster and V. Paul Marston make these relevant comments:

The prime point is that the election of the church is a corporate rather than an individual thing. It is not that individuals are in the church because they are elect, it is rather that they are elect because they are in the church, which is the body of the elect One. Ruth was not chosen to become an Israelite, but in becoming an Israelite she partook of Israel's election. A Christian is not chosen to become part of Christ's body, but in becoming part of Christ's body he partakes of Christ's election.[18]

There is plenty to think about in these words. Hopefully, there is enough obvious truth to reinforce the importance of seeing Christianity as a social faith. Original sin is inherently a desire for control that, if not mitigated by grace, will push believers apart. Christian spiritual formation is not just enhanced by community. It is broken and incomplete apart from the interaction of believers with one another and the world in the spirit of holy mutuality and love. Wesley would have appreciated *The Message* translation of Ecclesiastes 4:9-12:

> It's better to have a partner than go it alone.
> Share the work, share the wealth.
> And if one falls down, the other helps,
> But if there's no one to help, tough!
> Two in a bed warm each other.
> Alone, you shiver all night.
> By yourself, you're unprotected.
> With a friend you can face the worst.
> Can you round up a third?
> A three-stranded rope isn't easily snapped.

In the history of making disciples nothing Wesley did was more strategic than the creation of the societies (large congregation), the class meetings (small congregation), and the bands (intimate congregation). These were the engines of spiritual formation through which engagement with Jesus Christ grew richer and deeper. They formed a three-stranded rope that bound the Wesleyan movement together in support and

Belief #9

accountability. All effective makers of disciples will employ this same rope, a connection of grace and community in which Jesus builds his church.[19]

Questions for Discussion

1. Why would C. S. Lewis write such strong words about Jesus's command "Be ye perfect"?

2. How have you experienced the centrifugal force of sin?

3. What did Wesley mean when he said that Christianity is a "social religion"?

4. Richard Heitzenrater says that the purpose of the *bands* (smallest groups) was "to encourage faith working by love, that the love of God might be shed abroad in their hearts and lives." Where in your life do you receive or give such encouragement?

5. The class meetings became places where repentance was nurtured. Where does this happen in the church today?

6. What does it mean for the Christian faith to be personal but not private?

7. Why do many people consider "religion" a private matter?

8. How do you understand Witherington's statement, "What primarily happens at conversion is not Christ becoming a part of 'you' or being absorbed by 'you' but quite the reverse—you become a part of Christ's body: you become "in Christ"?

9. How might the three cords of Wesley's discipleship rope—the societies, the class meetings, and the bands—be a guide to disciple-making in the twenty-first century?

Belief #10

Entire Sanctification: Harmonizing Holy Intentions with Real Life

The Holy Spirit is sometimes called the Comforter. That term comes from Latin roots meaning "with strength." I remember a time years ago when the Comforter used me to give strength to someone dear to me. My wife and I had been married about ten years and were serving a congregation in the northern part of our annual conference. My sister-in-law was not yet married and lived in the southern part of Georgia. She was dating a young man who was employed in a children's home, which sounded good. But as she shared about him I became unsettled, feeling growing doubts that their relationship should go any further.

As it happened, at a point in time during those days I needed to travel south for a meeting. Driving toward the Florida line, an urge within, not characteristic of me at all, grew stronger and stronger: I should go out of my way and go speak to my sister-in-law about her relationship with that young man. So, I made my way to the town where she lived. She must have wondered what motivated my visit. I quickly got to the point: she needed to disengage from that relationship. Anyone who knows me understands that this was way out of my comfort zone.

121

I still recall the heart of what I communicated as I used this image: "You are a Porsche and he is an old Chevy." That cornball comparison seemed to communicate. I do not take credit for her eventual decision to stop that relationship, but to this day I am sure I did what I was supposed to do. She later met and married one of the best men I know, further confirming the providential value of my action. God's Spirit was reminding her of her true worth and potential, protecting against a relationship that could block her from abundant life.

Coming to the conclusion of this look at Wesley's interpretation of scriptural Christianity, I want to cooperate again with the Comforter. It would be all too natural to reach this point of considering the high calling of sanctification/holiness and for readers, regardless of how positive their self-image might otherwise be, to think, *This is way beyond me. Spiritually I am an old Chevy. Sanctification is for spiritual Porsches.*

This brings to mind a story from the beginnings of Alcoholics Anonymous. Dr. Bob Smith and Bill Wilson (Dr. Bob and Bill W.) went to a hospital in Akron, Ohio, and asked if there might be an alcoholic patient on which they could try their new method of achieving sobriety. They were put in touch with Bill D., a well-known attorney and city councilman. He had just come to the hospital with DTs, had blackened the eyes of two nurses, and was strapped down tight to a hospital bed. It was not his first such trip.

Dr. Bob and Bill W. explained their approach and their own experiences of being able to stay sober as a result. Bill D. was not impressed, expressing his belief that his case was too terrible. "You don't have to sell me religion, either," he said. "I was at one time a deacon in the church and I still believe in God. But I guess he doesn't believe much in me."[1]

Jesus knew what was naturally in a person (John 2:25). He didn't believe in people apart from the influence of God's grace. But in fellowship with God, Jesus plainly said, "All things are possible" (Matt 19:26). It was that kind of faith that undergirded Wesley's invitation for whosoever will to come and begin a journey toward reclaiming what the Creator sees in them and what can be reclaimed by grace.

> *John Wesley said the reason God raised up the people called Methodist in America was to spread scriptural holiness and to reform the continent.*

John Wesley said the reason God raised up the people called Methodist in America was to spread scriptural holiness and to reform the continent. Such an ambitious purpose statement is uniquely Methodist and clearly not for wimps. This conjunctive calling reflects *roots* of serious abiding in Christ, including the concepts of Christian perfection and entire sanctification. Reforming the continent anticipated the *wings* of intentional engagement with the world.

As are all United Methodist candidates for Elder's orders, at my ordination I was asked the so-called historic questions of Wesley that include: Are you going on to perfection? Do you expect to be made perfect in love in this life? Are you earnestly striving after perfection in love?[2] Those kinds of questions raise more questions. We will consider some of the obvious issues raised by terms such as perfection and entire sanctification. The Wesleyan goal was not just an understanding of ideas. The goal was engagement with and participation in what these terms represent. With God, Wesley was convinced, it is possible!

Did Wesley Teach Sinless Perfection?

The simple answer to that question is: no. Ignorance and the limits of the mind alone prevent human perfection as the term is normally used. Too, Wesley recognized the inevitability of failing to do all the good we might have done, especially when holy love is your standard.

In "Repentance of Believers," he takes note that the pious "Archbishop Ussher, after all his labours for God, cried out, almost with his dying breath, 'Lord forgive me for my sins of omission.'"[3]

To make absolute moral perfection the goal of holiness is setting an unreachable goal.

Expecting sinless perfection in an unqualified sense is living in denial of human reality. It brings to mind the story of a holy man who spent thirty years by himself on a mountain. When at last he came down, he said, "I have not thought about a woman in thirty years." A witness to this event later noted, "Isn't it interesting that was the first thing he said!" To make absolute moral perfection the goal of holiness is setting an unreachable goal.

Did Not Wesley Call People to Live Above Sin?

Wesley did call people to live above sin. What did he mean? To borrow from Bill Clinton, it all depends on what "sin" is. Wesley identified sin in two ways. He spoke of sins of omission, involuntary failure, as sin "improperly so called." He also spoke about sin in a more closely defined fashion. Sin "properly so called" is "a voluntary transgression of a known law."[4] In the first sense of the word, as we have just seen, Wesley clearly rejected "sinlessness." However, in the second sense, the voluntary transgression of a known law, Wesley did endorse what could sound like sinlessness (qualified) in the life of a reborn believer.

In "The Great Privilege of Those That Are Born of God" we hear Wesley explain his meaning: "By 'sin' I here understand outward sin, according to the plain, common acceptation of the word: an actual, voluntary 'transgression of the law'; of the revealed, written law of God; of any commandment of God acknowledged to be such at the time that it is transgressed."[5]

Wesley believed God's grace could enable a believer to "keep" him- or herself from such disobedience.

Consider the subject in regard to other matters of faithfulness and purity. An obvious place for comparison is marriage. Have you ever attended a wedding where the vows said, "Will you be faithful most of the time? Do you promise to love unless a better offer comes along?" It brings to mind the observation of the former secretary general of the United Nations Dag Hammerschold, who wrote, "He who wants to keep his garden tidy doesn't reserve a plot for weeds."[6]

Recently there was an article on the front page of a local newspaper addressing issues in our county jail. Maintaining order and safety in a day when members of different gangs end up in jail together has presented new challenges. Apparently some inmates have complained that the rules are too tough. The director of the jail recalled one woman suing the jail because she felt her sister was mistreated. He quotes the woman as saying, "Those jailers didn't treat my sister right and when my children grow up and go to jail I want them treated better."[7] Her anxiety would be humorous if it didn't have a strong element of painful reality in it. That profoundly sad truth recognized, is such inevitability, for lack of a better word, inevitable? Yet don't we essentially say that our children will have no choice but to grow up as voluntary breakers of God's known laws? Wesley believed the scriptural expectations for believers were higher than that.

What Did Wesley Mean by "Entire Sanctification/Christian Perfection"?

Wesley described entire sanctification, saying, "It is love excluding sin; love filling the heart, taking up the whole capacity of the soul."[8] Prominent Wesley scholar Ken Collins writes that entire sanctification is "holy love reigning in the heart, . . . love replacing sin, holy love conquering every vile passion and temper."[9] John Peters, in *Christian Perfection and American Methodism*, adds these helpful thoughts:

> "Entire sanctification," he [Wesley] said, ". . . is neither more nor less than pure love—love expelling sin and governing both the heart and life." And this is what he preached: "It is love excluding sin; love filling the heart, taking up the whole capacity of the soul. . . . For as long as love takes up the whole heart, what room is there for sin therein." Here in Wesley is the explicit teaching of the "expulsive power of a new affection." But again Wesley does not contend for a term: "Call this the destruction or suspension of sin, it is a glorious work."[10]

Entire sanctification means that the *being* or the presence of rebellion has been expelled much as light expels darkness.

Entire sanctification means that the being or the presence of rebellion has been expelled much as light expels darkness.

Yes, this sounds like territory reserved for spiritual Olympians. It is instructive and necessary at this point to understand the relationship between entire sanctification and Christian maturity. The word *entire* can be misleading. *Entire*, while it speaks of purity, does not speak of maturity. Jesus had a pure heart yet he matured as he grew. Wesley confirms, "So that how much soever any man hath attained, or in how high a degree soever he is perfect, he hath still need to 'grow in grace,' and daily to advance in the knowledge and love of God his Savior."[11]

Why Bother with Christian Perfection?

Wesley believed entire sanctification was a scriptural doctrine. God, he was convinced, will make possible all that God commands as his renewed children walk by faith. It is interesting that Wesley did not claim this experience for himself. Very likely he could foresee the consequences had he written a book entitled *A Plain Account of MY Christian Perfection.* Still, he did not back away from proclaiming entirely sanctifying grace.

"Reasonable enthusiast" that he was, Wesley also understood the practical impact of enthusiastically (in-God, in-Christ) seeking the highest goal. I recall seeing this sermon title in a church bulletin, "I Love You With Half My Heart." Did Jesus tell us to be satisfied with that?

Jesus called us to something great, a call that begins with grace in the heart, with roots, which then empowers the wings of love of God and neighbor in daily life. Crazy, impossible as it may strike some people, Wesley believed it was God's goal for humankind. To sincerely seek it was to make way for the incoming tide of the Holy Spirit who has power to "raise all the boats" in our lives.

The Ultimate Conjunction: Inward and Outward Holiness

I have no recollection of hearing John Wesley's name until I went to college. As I began to learn about his life and ministry what impressed me most was the balance he maintained between the inner and outer life of a Christian. The "warm heart" and the "outstretched hand" were both important. More than forty years and much learning later, it is still this balance I find most attractive and amazing.

Inward Holiness

Wesley could declare with confidence, "How great a thing it is to be a Christian, to be a real, inward, scriptural Christian! Conformed in heart and life to the will of God! Who is sufficient for these things? None, unless he be born of God."[12] Real, inward, scriptural, conformed (in heart and life to the will of God); these are adjectives that for Wesley identify the heart of authentic Christianity.

Writing in 1771 Wesley expressed concern that Methodists not forget the foundation of genuine religion: "The most prevailing fault among the Methodists is to be *too outward* in religion. We are continually forgetting that the kingdom of God is *within us*."[13] Otherwise, he affirmed, actions can flow from unworthy motives. "Yea, suppose a person of this amiable character to do much good wherever he is, to feed the hungry, clothe the naked, relieve the stranger, the sick, the prisoner, yes, and to save many souls from death: it is possible he may still fall far short of that holiness without which he cannot see the Lord."[14]

In the last year of his life, in a sermon later titled "On Living Without God," Wesley affirms the importance of what he termed right *tempers*, saying of so-called Christians, "unless they have new senses, ideas, passions, tempers, they are no Christians! However just, true, or merciful they may be, they are but atheists still."[15] *Tempers* are inner dispositions capable by grace of expressing the character of God. Fowler, writing about the development of faith, uses the term *affections* in the same sense that Wesley used *tempers*, identifying them as "(a) *deep-going, pervasive, and long-lasting set of fundamental dispositions of the heart.*"[16]

The transformation of the heart is at the core of the renewal of God's image.

Intentions are a fundamental way in which perfection, as Wesley understood it, is experienced. Steve Harper, Wesley scholar and spiritual formation authority, shares a simple but classic example of the nature of pure intentions. When his children were very young, they each at some point in time got the bright idea of bringing their mommy some flowers. The fact that the flowers were picked from the flower bed mommy had carefully cultivated was of no concern to them. Never mind that such flowers might even have come from the neighbor's flower beds. Their one desire was to show their love for their mommy and please her. So, in they would come with flowers, weeds, and dirt. With cherubic faces they would exclaim, "Mommy, we love you!"

What did mommy do? Did she reject the messy offering? Did she refuse to accept the gift because they had been stolen from her bed or the bed of a neighbor? Of course not! With the eyes of love she would take her nicest vase and proudly display this gift of pure love for all to see. There would be an appropriate time later on for a lesson in flower picking. Harper comments,

> So it is with God. He accepts our intentions. He sees our motives. It has to be this way, for in the light of his impeccable holiness even our best actions fall short. The Bible puts it this way, even our best actions look like filthy rags in comparison to God. We cannot hope to match him in actions, but we can be one with him in motive. Our controlling desire can be to do his will on earth as it is in heaven. God knows whether or not that is our intention, and when it is, he calls it "perfect" even though it comes packaged with some weeds and dirt.[17]

The transformation of the heart is at the core of the renewal of God's image. The renewal of our minds (Rom 12:2) by grace and the conforming of our inner self to "the attitude that was in Christ Jesus" (Phil 2:5) is central to "inner holiness," the kingdom of God within us.

Outward Holiness

Holiness, while not a verb, is an active principle. As a result genuine holiness is going to include outward expressions of faith expressed through love. Galatians 5:6 reminds us, "Being circumcised doesn't matter in Christ Jesus, but faith working through love does matter." Believing as he did in conversion as a significant inner change, Wesley would not avoid the necessary consequent expectation of changed behavior. Such altered behavior would be part of outward holiness. In the early years of my ministry there was a widely read book entitled *Journey Inward, Journey Outward.* John Wesley would have liked such a conjunctive title. Christian holiness is empowered by the Holy One whom we see most clearly in Jesus Christ. Like a heartbeat, the journey of faith constantly receives life from Christ and sends out life from Christ. Receiving necessarily comes first, but outwardly expending what has been received is the utterly natural result of living in the rhythm of faith. Wesley exhorted his hearers to seek a significant inward change of heart, a journey inward. As we shall see he also modeled the outward journey of seeking to meet the needs of the helpless, provide education to elevate the common person, and work for justice for the oppressed. A fair question sometimes put to those who are making the inward journey is, "What difference does it make to anyone else?" Wesley was determined that the spiritual formation structures of various Wesleyan groups not become holy huddles or spiritual dead ends. Wesleyan Christianity is a life of seeking both a regular inflow of grace and a constant outflow of holy love. Wesley would call this plain old Bible Christianity.

Motives for Love

As a parent, pastor, and person seeking to follow Jesus, I have learned that knowing how to love someone, especially knowing how to help another person, calls for discernment and wisdom. "Love" without banks can become a swamp that enables others to continue in dependent and even destructive behaviors.

It is common for Christians to be drawn either toward pietistic, evangelical expressions of faith or a prophetic, justice-seeking focus. As the Wesley Covenant Service affirms of various ministries, "some are suitable to our inclinations and interests, others are contrary to both. In some we may please Christ and please ourselves....But then there are other works wherein to please Christ is to deny ourselves."[18] To "please Christ" is the motive that, as love often does, can move us out of our comfort zones. Works of love can *please* Christ as he identifies with the needy. Wesley exhorts:

> He doth good, to the uttermost of his power, even to the bodies of all men. He rejoices to "deal his bread to the hungry," and to "cover the naked with a garment." Is any a stranger? He takes him in, and relieves him according to his necessities. Are any sick or in prison? He visits them, and administers such help as they stand most in need of. And all this he does, not as unto man, but remembering him that hath said, "Inasmuch as ye have done it unto one of the least of these my brethren, ye have done it unto me."[19]

St. Augustine advised, "Love God and do what you like," knowing that real love for God would result in real outward holiness. It comes as no surprise, then, that this is the first and greatest commandment. Love God and you are highly likely to *do* (outwardly) what God likes.

John Wesley: A Person Who Walked His Talk

As a young Christian, I remember reading about Wesley in his eighties, walking the snow-covered streets of London soliciting money to feed the poor. Although I do not recall the source of that report, it is consistent with his character as I have learned of it since. For example, long before the term "micro loan" was invented, early in the revival, Wesley led the London society to collect "lending stock," out of which loans of up to twenty shillings (one pound) were made to those who needed "a present supply of money" for such purposes as "to carry on their business." In the first year of this endeavor, 250 people were provided with this type of loan. One of the success stories of this program was a bookseller named James Lackington. Beginning with a few dozen books, Lackington eventually became a wealthy man, the proprietor of one of London's largest bookstores. A Methodist at the time he received the loan, Lackington eventually left the Methodists. In his memoirs, he reports feeling Wesley was charitable to an extreme, seldom denying help to any poor person who asked for it. With some astonishment, Lackington recalled Wesley could not walk the few yards from his study to the pulpit without giving out coins to the poor old people of his society.[20] Lackington apparently liked the "gain all you can so you can save all you can" parts of Wesley's recommendations for stewardship. When it came to "so you can give all you can," it seems that two out of three was good enough. In his sermon "The More Excellent Way," Wesley writes of himself:

> One of (the young men at Oxford) had thirty pounds a year. He lived on twenty-eight and gave away forty shillings. The next year receiving sixty pounds, he still lived on twenty-eight, and gave away two and thirty. The third year he received ninety pounds, and gave away sixty-two. The fourth year he received a hundred and twenty pounds. Still he lived on twenty-eight, and gave to the poor ninety-two. Was not this a more excellent way?[21]

In his challenging book *Freedom of Simplicity*, contemporary spiritual formation author Richard Foster echoes Wesley's teaching and practice of "wealth management." "The theology of wealth says, 'I give so that I can get.' Christian simplicity says, 'I get so that I can give.' The difference is profound."[22]

"Come Up Higher"

John Wesley wrote to Miss March, a woman of wealth and education, guiding her to "Go and see the poor and sick in their own poor little hovels. Take up your cross, woman! Remember the faith! Jesus went before you, and will go with you." He minced no words in directing her to "Creep in among these in spite of dirt and of an hundred disgusting circumstances," and "do not confine your conversation to genteel and elegant people."[23] In a follow-up letter, Wesley clarified his meaning, encouraging her:

to visit the poor, the widow, the sick, the fatherless in their affliction; and this, although they should have nothing to recommend
them but that they are bought with the blood of Christ. It is true
this is not pleasing to the flesh and blood. There are a thousand
circumstances usually attending it which shock the delicacy of our
nature, or rather of our education. But yet the blessing which follows this labour of love will more than balance the cross.[24]

Wesley and the Methodists expressed the love of Christ in numerous
outward ways:

• medical dispensaries
• houses for older widows
• teaching children at the Foundery
• the Kingswood School near Bristol
• ministry to prisoners
• early manifestations of Sunday schools
• regular distribution of financial support for the poor (the class
  meetings included offerings for benevolent purposes)
• micro-loan program

With regard to justice, Wesley was an ardent opponent of slavery.
His final letter was written to William Wilberforce, a member of Parlia-
ment, urging him to continue his abolitionist efforts: "O be not weary
of well doing! Go on, in the name of God and in the power of His
might, till even American slavery (the vilest that ever saw the sun) shall
vanish away before it."[25]

Even in preparing for death and burial, John Wesley was passionate
about loving his neighbor. He stipulated that he be buried wrapped in
wool rather than a finer cloth. Six poor men should be enlisted to carry
his body and each be given twenty shillings. The whole chapel was to be
draped in black, the material carefully chosen so that it could be re-used
to provide "decent dresses" for sixty poor women.

In the early years of the revival (1739–1746), Wesley preached
more than one hundred sermons on separate texts from the Sermon

on the Mount (Matt 5–7). Outler notes, "Maybe more than anywhere else...this...displays Wesley's distinctive concern for integration and balance—between the faith that justifies and the faith that works by love."[26] In the thirteenth of his series of thirteen sermons on these chapters, Wesley calls disciples to action, to "come up higher":

> Over and above all this, are you zealous of good works? Do you, as you have time, do good to all men? Do you feed the hungry and clothe the naked, and visit the fatherless and widow in their affliction? Do you visit those that are sick? Relieve them that are in prison? Is any a stranger and you take him in? *Friend, come up higher....* Does he enable you to bring sinners from darkness to light, from the power of Satan unto God? Then go and learn what thou hast so often taught, "By grace ye are saved, through faith." Not by works of righteousness which we have done, but of his own mercy he saveth us." Learn to hang naked upon the cross of Christ, counting all thou hast done but dung and dross [emphasis mine].[27]

Discipleship: A Balanced, Serving Life

Many years later (1784) in his sermon "On Perfection" Wesley again affirms the balance of inner and outer holiness that he sought to encourage throughout his ministry: "What is then the perfection of which man is capable while he dwells in a corruptible body?...The first branch of it is the love of God: and as he that loves God loves his brother also....Perfection is another name for universal holiness—inward and outward righteousness—holiness of life arising from holiness of heart."[28] This was the holy, grace-enabled balance to which John Wesley called all who would listen.

Not long ago I found myself caught up in a sense of God's high calling. It was not in church but while watching a YouTube video in which Celine Dion, with the help of technology, sings a duet with Frank Sinatra. The song was one of Sinatra's big hits, "All the Way." As this exquisite duet unfolded, I felt its application to sanctification.

It is so true that when another person loves you, it's useless unless he or she loves you whole heartedly.

This very emotive song goes on to describe a kind of love that is deeper than the ocean and taller than the tallest trees. It is a love that remains faithful in good times and bad, even if the pathway ahead is uncertain. It is akin to God's agape love, the love we saw in Jesus, the love of Jesus in whom we are called to abide. Such love presses on...all the way.

Hear John Wesley's invitation:

Friend, come up higher...

Questions for Discussion

1. How do you initially respond to the idea of Christian perfection?

2. In what ways would you identify with Bishop Usher whose final words included, "Lord, forgive me for my sins of omission"?

3. What do you think about the inevitability of sin "properly so called"?

4. Have you ever known someone who seemed to have a purified heart? Explain.

5. Does entire sanctification mean that a person has no room for growth? If there is room for growth, what does "entire" imply?

6. Why was Wesley so concerned that faith be built on the foundation of *inward* holiness? Why was he so concerned to encourage faith working by love?

Notes

Introduction

1. N. T. Wright, *Simply Christian: Why Christianity Makes Sense* (San Francisco: Harper Collins, 2006), 3.

2. For a detailed description of the Willow Creek discoveries see Greg L. Hawkins and Cally Parkinson, *Move: What 1000 Churches Reveal About Spiritual Growth* (Grand Rapids: Zondervan, 2001).

3. Keven Vanhoozer, *The Drama of Doctrine* (Louisville: Westminister John Knox, 2005) 44.

4. Ibid. 44.

5. Anonymous, "I Sought the Lord," *The United Methodist Hymnal* (Nashville: The United Methodist Publishing House, 1989), 341.

6. Philip Yancey, *What Good Is God: In Search of a Faith That Matters* (New York: FaithWords, 2010), 104.

7. John Wesley, *Sermons I (1–33),* ed. Albert C. Outler, vol. 1 of The Bicentennial Edition of the Works of John Wesley (Nashville: Abingdon Press, 1984), 27–28.

8. Albert C. Outler, *Theology in the Wesleyan Spirit* (Nashville: Discipleship Resources, 1975), 13.

9. John Wesley, *The Letters of the Rev. John Wesley,* ed. John Telford, vol. 6 (London: Epworth, 1951), 326–27.

10. Handley Moule, *Charles Simeon: Pastor of a Generation* (Fearn-Ross-Shire, Great Britain: Christian Focus, 1997), 80.

11. A. W. Tozer, *That Incredible Christian* (Milton Keynes, UK: Authentic Lifestyle, 2001), 34, 65.

12. Paul Wesley Chilcote, *Recapturing the Wesley's Vision* (Downers Grove, IL: Intervarsity, 2004), 19.

13. Richard Heitzenrater, *The Elusive Mr. Wesley*, 2nd ed. (Nashville: Abingdon Press, 1984), 28–29.

14. Phillips Brooks, *Lectures on Preaching* (Grand Rapids: Baker Books, 1969), 5.

15. Ibid., 126.

16. G. K. Chesterton, *Autobiography, Collected Works,* vol. 16 (San Francisco: Ignatius, 1988), 212.

1. Scripture Is Our Primary Source

1. Richard Heitzenrater, *Wesley and the People Called Methodist* (Nashville: Abingdon Press, 2013), 42.

2. John Wesley, *Explanatory Notes Upon the New Testament* (London: Epworth, 1952), 9.

3. John Wesley, *The Works of John Wesley*, ed. Thomas Jackson, vol. 5 (Grand Rapids: Baker Books, 2007), 3.

4. Wesley in Jackson, *Works* 8, 349.

5. Wesley in Telford, *Letters 1*, 285.

6. Wesley in Telford, *Letters 8*, 191–92.

7. Charles Spurgeon, "The Lover of God's Soul Filled With Peace" (sermon, Metropolitan Tabernacle, Newington, January 22, 1888), http://www.spurgeongems.org/vols34-36/chs2004.pdf.

8. Wesley in Jackson, *Works 11*, 484.

9. Joel B. Green, "Scripture in the Church," in *Wesleyan Tradition: A Paradigm for Renewal*, ed. Paul W. Chilcote (Nashville: Abingdon Press, 2002), 42.

10. Wesley, *Explanatory Notes Upon the New Testament,* 8–9.

11. Wesley, *Explanatory Notes Upon the New Testament,* 794.

12. Heitzenrater, *The Elusive Mr. Wesley,* 359.

13. Wesley in Outler, *Sermons 1,* 105.

14. Emile Calliet, *Journey Into Light* (Grand Rapids: Zondervan, 1968), 12.

15. James Thomson, "The City of Dreadful Night," *The City of Dreadful Night: And Other Poems* (London: Reeves and Turner, 1880), 54-55.

16. Calliet, *Journey Into Light*, 16.

17. Ibid.

18. Ibid., 17.

19. Ibid., 18.

20. Outler, *Theology in the Wesleyan Spirit*, 4.

21. John Telford, *The Life of John Wesley* (New York: Eaton and Mains, 1886), 315.

22. W. Stephen Gunter, et al., "The Quadrilateral and the 'Middle Way,'" *Wesley and the Quadrilateral: Renewing the Conversation* (Nashville: Abingdon Press, 1997), 41.

23. Henry Rack, *Reasonable Enthusiast: John Wesley and the Rise of Methodism* (Nashville: Abingdon Press, 1989), 351.

2. Reason, Tradition, and Experience Help Us Understand Scripture

1. J. D. Salinger, *The Catcher in the Rye* (New York: Little Brown, 1951), 25.

2. John Wesley, *Sermons II (34–70),* ed. Albert C. Outler, vol. 2 of The Bicentennial Edition of the Works of John Wesley (Nashville: Abingdon Press, 1985), 588.

3. Wesley in Outler, *Sermons II,* 588.

4. Wesley in Telford, *Letters,* 5:164.

5. John Wesley, *Sermons IV (114–151)*, ed. Albert C. Outler, vol. 4 of The Bicentennial Edition of the Works of John Wesley (Nashville: Abingdon Press, 1987), 172–73.

6. Thomas C. Oden, *John Wesley's Scriptural Christianity* (Grand Rapids: Zondervan, 1994), 67.

7. Ibid., 66.

8. John Pearson, "Great Anglican Divines (5) John Pearson—Bishop of Chester, 1613–1668," quoted in David C. C. Watson, *Cross Way,* Winter 1986, no. 23, www.churchsociety.org/crossway/documents/Cway-023-JohnPearson.pdf, November 17, 2010 (accessed September 9, 2015).

9. Ted Campbell in Gunter et al., "The Interpretive Role of Tradition," *Wesley and the Quadrilateral: Renewing the Conversation,* 73.

10. Wesley in Telford, *Letters,* 7:47.

11. Luke Tyerman, *The Life and Times of the Rev. John Wesley* (New York: Burt Franklin, 1872), 3:519.

12. Wesley in Outler, *Sermons II,* 50.

13. Randy Maddox, *Responsible Grace* (Nashville: Kingswood, 1994), 128.

14. Oden, *John Wesley's Scriptural Christianity,* 90.

15. Colin Williams, *John Wesley's Theology Today* (Nashville: Abingdon Press, 1960), 112.

16. Ibid., 112.

17. John Wesley, *Sermons III (71–114),* ed. Albert C. Outler, vol. 3 of The Bicentennial Edition of the Works of John Wesley (Nashville: Abingdon Press, 1986), 497.

18. Randy Maddox in Gunter et al., "The Enriching Role of Experience," *Wesley and the Quadrilateral,* 123.

19. Thomas C. Oden, *Doctrinal Standards in the Wesleyan Tradition* (Grand Rapids: Zondervan, 1988), 117.

20. N. T. Wright, *Scripture and the Authority of God* (San Francisco: HarperOne, 2013), 102.

21. N. T. Wright, *The Last Word: Beyond the Bible Wars to a New Understanding of Scripture* (San Francisco: HarperSanFrancisco, 2005), 101.

22. William J. Abraham, *Waking From Doctrinal Amnesia* (Nashville: Abingdon Press, 1995), 63–64.

23. N. T. Wright, *Scripture and the Authority of God,* 101.

3. Grace Is the Necessary Glue of All Discipleship

1. Maddox, *Responsible Grace,* 19.

2. Ibid.

3. Ibid., 255.

4. Wesley in Jackson, *Works,* 6:512.

5. Ibid, 7:187.

6. William J. Abraham, *Wesley For Armchair Theologians* (Louisville: Westminister John Knox, 2005), 20.

7. Wesley in Outler, *Sermons II,* 42.

8. Maddox, *Responsible Grace,* 18.

9. John Wesley, *John Wesley's Sermons: An Anthology,* eds. Albert C. Outler and Richard P. Heitzenrater (Nashville: Abingdon Press, 1991), 167.

10. John Wesley, *Explanatory Notes Upon the New Testament,* 912.

11. Wesley in Telford, *Letters,* 4:298.

12. Wesley in Jackson, *Works,* 12:68.

13. Wesley in Outler, *Sermons I,* 219–20.

14. George Buttrick, ed., *The Interpreter's Bible* (Nashville: Abingdon Press, 1952), 8:301.

15. Maddox, *Responsible Grace,* 132.

16. Greggory S. Clapper, *As If the Heart Mattered: A Wesleyan Spirituality* (Nashville: Upper Room, 1997), 19ff; Greggory S. Clapper, *The Renewal of the Heart is the Mission of the Church: Wesley's Heart Religion In the Twenty-First Century* (Eugene, OR: Cascade, 2010), 68ff.

17. Theodore Runyon, *The New Creation: John Wesley's Theology Today* (Nashville: Abingdon Press, 1998), 146ff.

18. Wesley in Outler, *Sermons II,* 185.

19. Wesley in Telford, *Letters,* 5:289.

20. John Wesley, *Explanatory Notes Upon the New Testament,* 859–60.

21. Ibid.

22. Ibid.

23. Clapper, *The Renewal of the Heart,* 6–7.

24. Ian Leitch, *Life Before Death* (Larkspur, CO: Green Acres, 2007), 100.

4. Prevenient Grace

1. J. C. Ryle, *Holiness: It's Nature, Hindrances, Difficulties, and Roots* (Peabody, MA: Hendrickson Publishers, reprint 2007 [1877]), 13.

2. Quoted in Brennan Manning, *Abba's Child: The Cry of the Heart For Intimate Belonging* (Colorado Spring: Navpress, 1994), 11.

3. Wright, *Scripture and the Authority of God,* 85.

4. Alan Bloom, *The Closing of the American Mind: How Education*

Has Failed Democracy and Impoverished the Souls of Today's Students (New York: Simon and Schuster, 1987), 197.

5. Wesley in Jackson, *Works*, 9:194.

6. Cited in Kenneth J. Collins, *The Theology of John Wesley: Holy Love and the Shape of Grace* (Nashville: Abingdon Press, 2007), 64.

7. John Ortberg, *The Me I Want to Be: Becoming God's Best Version of You* (Grand Rapids: Zondervan, 2009), 145–46.

8. Wesley in Outler and Heitzenrater, *John Wesley's Sermons*, 326.

9. Ibid,. 328.

10. Ibid., 333.

11. Outler, *Theology in the Wesleyan Spirit*, 36; Rack, *Reasonable Enthusiast*, 280.

12. Oden, *John Wesley's Scriptural Christianity*, 175.

13. Wright, *Simply Christian*, 25.

14. Collins, *The Theology of John Wesley*, 152.

15. Outler, *John Wesley* (New York: Oxford University Press, 1964), 152.

16. Wesley in Outler and Heitzenrater, *John Wesley's Sermons*, 50.

17. Ibid., 490–91.

18. Wesley in Jackson, *Works*, 7:187–88.

5. Repentance

1. Wesley in Outler, *Sermons*, 4:397; see also Wesley in Outler, *Sermons*, 3:205.

2. Wesley in Outler and Heitzenrater, *John Wesley's Sermons*, 124ff.

3. Ibid., 125.

4. Ibid., 488.

5. Wesley in Telford, *Letters*, 2:268.

6. C. S. Lewis, *Mere Christianity* (London: Fontana Books, 1955), 122–23.

7. Wesley in Outler and Heitzenrater, *John Wesley's Sermons*, 45, 117.

8. Outler, *John Wesley*, 137.

9. Wesley in Outler and Heitzenrater, *John Wesley's Sermons*, 489.

10. Ibid., 490–91.

11. Outler, *John Wesley*, 137.

12. Wesley in Outler and Heitzenrater, *John Wesley's Sermons*, 376.

13. Outler, *John Wesley*, 178–179.

14. Richard P. Heitzenrater, *Wesley and the People Called Methodist* (Nashville: Abingdon Press, 1995), 138.

15. Outler, *John Wesley*, 178.

16. Heitzenrater, *Wesley and the People Called Methodist*, 138–39.

17. Collins, *The Theology of John Wesley*, 158.

18. Ken Gire, *Windows of the Soul: Experiencing God in New Ways* (Grand Rapids: Zondervan, 1996), 215.

6. Justification

1. Philip Yancey, *What's So Amazing About Grace?* (Grand Rapids: Zondervan, 1997), 45; Collins, *The Theology of John Wesley*, 192.

2. Wesley in Outler and Heitzenrater, *John Wesley's Sermons*, 336.

3. Ibid., 115.

4. Outler, *John Wesley*, 136–37.

5. Charles Wesley in Thomas Jackson, *The Journal of the Rev. Charles Wesley* (Grand Rapids: Baker Books, 1980), 1:82.

6. Wesley in Outler, *Sermons I*, 454, 462.

7. Stephen Gunter, *The Limits of Love Divine: John Wesley's Response to Antinomianism and Enthusiasm* (Nashville: Kingswood Books, 1989), 114.

8. William H. Willimon, *This We Believe: The Core of Wesleyan Faith and Practice* (Nashville: Abingdon Press, 2010), 93.

9. Williams, *John Wesley's Theology Today*, 71–72.

10. Clapper, *The Renewal of the Heart*, 6–7.

11. Outler, *John Wesley*, 189.

7. Initial Sanctification

1. Heitzenrater, *Wesley and the People Called Methodist*, 159.

2. Wesley in Jackson, *Works*, 1:23.

3. Ibid., 1:103.

4. Kenneth J. Collins, *John Wesley: A Theological Journey* (Nashville: Abingdon Press, 2003), 133ff.

5. Wesley in Outler, *Sermons IV,* 35.

6. Kenneth Boa, e-mail message to author, August 11, 2015.

7. Wesley in Telford, *Letters,* 7:361–362.

8. Maddox, *Responsible Grace,* 168.

9. Joseph P. Blank, *19 Steps Up the Mountain: The Story of the DeBolt Family* (New York: Jove Publications, 1976), 48–49.

10. Collins, *John Wesley: A Theological Journey,* 132.

11. Wesley in Jackson, *Works,* 8:276.

12. Wesley in Outler, *Sermons I,* 141.

13. Wesley in Outler, *Sermons III,* 497.

14. Ibid.

15. Wesley in Telford, *Letters,* 7:61.

16. Wesley in Outler, *Sermons II,* 193–94.

17. Wesley in Jackson, *Works,* 10:365–66.

18. Charles Wesley, "Blessed Be the Name of the Lord," 1739.

8. Holy Love

1. Woody Allen, "My Philosophy, *The New Yorker,* December 27, 1969, 26.

2. Philip Yancey, *The Jesus I Never Knew* (Grand Rapids: Zondervan, 2002), 80.

3. Dallas Willard, *Renovation of the Heart: Putting On the Character of Christ* (Colorado Springs: NavPress, 2002), 59.

4. Yancey, *What's So Amazing About Grace?,* 272.

5. Wesley in Outler, *Sermons I,* 432.

6. J. B. Phillips, *The Newborn Christian* (New York: Macmillan, 1978), 190.

7. John Wesley, *Explanatory Notes Upon the New Testament,* 711.

8. Wesley in Outler, *Sermons II,* 483–84.

9. Ibid., 107.

10. Rack, *Reasonable Enthusiast,* 360.

11. J. Wesley Bready, *England Before and After Wesley: The Evangeli-*

cal Revival and Social Reform (London: Hodder and Stoughton Limited, 1938), 19.

12. Ibid., 56–57.

13. Oden, *John Wesley's Scriptural Christianity,* 156.

14. Ibid., 93.

15. Wesley in Outler, *Sermons I,* 179.

16. Wesley in Outler, *Sermons IV,* 149.

17. James W. Fowler, *Becoming Adult, Becoming Christian: Adult Development and Christian Faith* (San Francisco: Harper and Row Publishers, 1984), 20.

18. Wesley in Outler, *Sermons I,* 139.

19. John L. Peters, *Christian Perfection and American Methodism* (Salem, OH: Schmul, 1995), 78.

20. Peters, *Christian Perfection and American Methodism,* 79.

21. C. S. Lewis, *The Weight of Glory and Other Addresses* (Grand Rapids: William B. Eerdmans, 1949), 1.

22. Wesley in Outler, *Sermons II,* 482–83.

23. Wesley in Outler, *Sermons I,* 290ff.

24. Wesley in Outler, *Sermons IV,* 354.

25. Wesley in Outler, *Sermons I,* 220.

26. Ibid., 413–14.

27. Wesley in Outler, *Sermons III,* 74.

28. Ibid., 313.

29. Wesley in Outler, *Sermons I,* 139.

9. We Are Better Together

1. Charles Swindoll, *The Tale of the Tardy Oxcart* (Nashville: Word Publishing, 1998), 401.

2. John Wesley, *Explanatory Notes Upon the New Testament,* 676.

3. Dallas Willard, *The Divine Conspiracy: Rediscovering Our Hidden Life in God* (San Francisco: HarperSanFrancisco, 1998), 129.

4. Wesley in Outler, *Sermons II,* 158.

5. Wesley in Outler, *Sermons I,* 533–34.

6. Ibid., 533.

7. Wesley in Telford, *Letters,* 7:154.

8. Heitzenrater: *Wesley and the People Called Methodist,* 20.

9. Ibid., 91, 102.

10. Ibid., 105.

11. D. Michael Henderson, *John Wesley's Class Meeting: A Model for Making Disciples* (Nappanee, IN: Francis Asbury Press, 1997), 30.

12. Fowler, *Becoming Adult, Becoming Christian,* 126.

13. Wesley in Outler, *Sermons I,* 534.

14. Rack, *Reasonable Enthusiast,* 105.

15. Wesley in Outler, *Sermons I,* 533.

16. Wesley in Outler, *Sermons II,* 193.

17. Ben Witheringnton III, *A Shared Christian Life,* (Nashville: Abingdon Press, 2012), 21–22.

18. Roger T. Forster and V. Paul Marston, *God's Strategy in Human History* (Wheaton, IL: Tyndale, 1973), 136.

19. Note: British historian Henry Rack interestingly comments on the Wesley Covenant Service as an example of the integration of personal and social faith:

> What is characteristic of the Methodist rite is that it took the old Puritan individual covenant and made it a collective act of self-examination and renewal of vows and dedication to God, while using words still suitable for individual acceptance within the corporate act. It neatly expressed the Methodist sense of a personal pilgrimage in company with the society of the people of God. *Reasonable Enthusiast,* 413.

10. Entire Santification

1. Nancy O., "The Man on the Bed," barefootsworld.net, July 17, 2001, barefootsworld.net/aabilld-aa3.html (accessed September 7, 2015).

2. Wesley in Jackson, *Works,* 8:325.

3. Wesley in Outler, *Sermons I,* 343–44.

4. Wesley in Jackson, *Works,* 11:396.

5. Wesley in Outler *Sermons I,* 436.

6. Dag Hammerschold, *Markings* (New York: Alfred A. Knopf, 1964), 15.

7. Pete Skiba, "Director: Tough Rules Required to Maintain Order," *Albany Herald* 120, no. 335 (September 28, 2012), 1.

8. Wesley in Outler, *Sermons II*, 160.

9. Collins, *The Theology of John Wesley*, 298, 302.

10. Williams, *John Wesley's Theology Today*, 183.

11. Wesley in Outler, *Sermons II*, 104–5.

12. Wesley in Outler, *Sermons IV*, 121–22.

13. Wesley in Telford, *Letters*, 5:289.

14. Wesley in Outler, *Sermons IV*, 147.

15. Ibid., 175.

16. Fowler, *Becoming Adult, Becoming Christian*, 118.

17. Steve Harper, *John Wesley's Message for Today* (Grand Rapids: Zondervan, 1983), 95–96.

18. Jeren Rowel, "Wesley Covenant Service—1998, Adapted from John Wesley," *Wesley Center Online*, http://wesley.nnu.edu/john-wesley/covenant-service-directions-for-renewing-our-covenant-with-god/wesley-covenant-service-1998-jeren-rowel/, (accessed September 6, 2015).

19. Wesley in Outler, *Sermons I*, 519.

20. Heitzenrater, *Wesley and the People Called Methodist*, 252.

21. Wesley in Outler, *Sermons III*, 275–76.

22. Richard J. Foster, *Freedom of Simplicity* (New York: Harper Paperbacks, 1981), 189.

23. Heitzenrater, *Wesley and the People Called Methodist*, 252.

24. Ibid., 252.

25. Wesley in Telford, *Letters*, 8:265.

26. Wesley in Outler, *Sermons I*, 695.

27. Ibid.

28. Wesley in Outler, *Sermons III*, 74–75.

Selected Bibliography

Primary Works of John and Charles Wesley

Davies, Rupert E., ed. *The Works of John Wesley*. Bicentennial ed. Vol. 9, *The Methodist Societies*, I: History, Nature, and Design. Nashville: Abingdon Press, 1989.

Jackson, Thomas, ed. *The Journal of Rev. Charles Wesley*. 2 vols. London: John Mason, 1949. Reprinted Grand Rapids: Baker Book House, 1980.

_____, ed. *The Works of John Wesley*. 14 vols. London: Wesleyan Book Room, 1872. Reprinted Grand Rapids: Baker Books, 2007.

Kimbrough, S. T., Jr. *A Song for the Poor: Hymns by Charles Wesley*. New York: Board of Global Ministry, 1993.

Outler, Albert C., ed. *John Wesley. The Library of Protestant Thought*. New York: Oxford University Press, 1964.

_____, ed. *The Works of John Wesley*. Bicentennial ed. Vol. 1–4, *Sermons*. Nashville: Abingdon Press, 1984–87.

Outler, Albert C., and Richard P. Heitzenrater, eds. *John Wesley's Sermons: An Anthology*. Nashville: Abingdon Press, 1991.

Sermons on Several Occasions by the Rev. John Wesley, A.M., 9th ed., 2 vols., 1824.

Telford, John, ed. *The Letters of the Rev. John Wesley*. 8 vols. London: Epworth Press, 1951.

Ward, W. Regindald, and Richard P. Heitzenrater, eds. *Explanatory Notes Upon the New Testament*. London: The Epworth Press, 1952. Reprint.

————. *A Plain Account of Christian Perfection*. Kansas City, MO: Beacon Hill Press, 1971.

————. *The Works of John Wesley*. Bicentennial ed. Vols. 18–24, *Journals and Diaries* I–VII. Nashville: Abingdon Press, 1988–97.

Secondary Works

Books

Abraham, William J. *Crossing the Threshold of Divine Revelation*. Grand Rapids: William B. Eerdmans Publishing Company, 2006.

————. *Waking from Doctrinal Amnesia: The Healing of Doctrine in the United Methodist Church*. Nashville: Abingdon Press, 1995.

————. *Wesley for Armchair Theologians*. Louisville: Westminster John Knox Press, 2005.

Bainton, Roland. *Here I Stand: A Life of Martin Luther*. Nashville: Abingdon Press, 1950.

Blank, Joseph P. *19 Steps Up the Mountain: The Story of the DeBolt Family*. New York: Jove Publications, 1976.

Bloom, Alan. *The Closing of the American Mind: How Higher Education Has Failed Democracy and Impoverished the Souls of Today's Students*. New York: Simon and Schuster, 1987.

Bready, J. Wesley. *England: Before and After Wesley (The Evangelical Revival and Social Reform)*. London: Hodder and Stoughton Limited, 1938.

Brooks, Phillips. *Lectures on Preaching*. Grand Rapids: Baker Book House, 1969.

Buttrick, George A. *The Interpreter's Bible*, Vol. 8. Nashville: Abingdon Press, 1952.

Cailliet, Emile. *Journey into Light*. Grand Rapids: Zondervan Publishing House, 1968.

Chilcote, Paul W. *Recapturing the Wesley's Vision.* Downers Grove, IL: InterVarsity Press, 2004.

_____. *The Wesleyan Tradition: A Paradigm for Renewal.* Nashville: Abingdon Press, 2002.

Clapper, Gregory S. *As If the Heart Mattered: A Wesleyan Spirituality.* Nashville: Upper Room Books, 1997.

_____. *The Renewal of the Heart Is the Mission of the Church: Wesley's Heart Religion in the Twenty-First Century.* Eugene, OR: Cascade Books, 2010.

Collected Works of G. K. Chesterton, Vol. 16: The Autobiography. San Francisco: Ignatius Press, 1988.

Collins, Kenneth J. *A Real Christian: The Life of John Wesley.* Nashville: Abingdon Press, 1999.

_____. *John Wesley: A Theological Journey.* Nashville: Abingdon Press, 2003.

_____. *The Scripture Way of Salvation: The Heart of John Wesley's Theology.* Nashville: Abingdon Press, 1997.

_____. *The Theology of John Wesley: Holy Love and the Shape of Grace.* Nashville: Abingdon Press, 2007.

Forster, Roger T., and V. Paul Marston. *God's Strategy in Human History.* Wheaton, IL: Tyndale House Publishers, 1973.

Foster, Richard J. *Freedom of Simplicity.* New York: Harper Paperbacks, 1981.

Fowler, James W. *Becoming Adult, Becoming Christian: Adult Development and Christian Faith.* San Francisco: Harper & Row Publishers, 1984.

Gire, Ken. *Windows of the Soul: Experiencing God in New Ways.* Grand Rapids: Zondervan Publishing House, 1996.

Gunter, W. Stephen. *The Limits of 'Love Divine': John Wesley's Response to Antinomianism and Enthusiasm.* Nashville: Kingswood Books, 1989.

Hammerschold, Dag. *Markings.* New York: Alfred A. Knofp, 1964.

Harper, Steve. *John Wesley's Message for Today.* Grand Rapids: Zondervan Publishing House, 1983.

Hawkins, Greg L., and Cally Parkinson. *Move: What 1,000 Churches Reveal About Spiritual Growth*. Grand Rapids: Zondervan, 2011.

Heitzenrater, Richard P. *The Elusive Mr. Wesley*, 2nd ed. Nashville: Abingdon Press, 2003.

_____. *Wesley and the People Called Methodist*. Nashville: Abingdon Press, 1995.

Henderson, D. Michael. *A Model for Making Disciples: John Wesley's Class Meeting*. Nappanee, IN: Francis Asbury Press, 1997.

Job, Rueben P. *Three Simple Rules: A Wesleyan Way of Living*. Nashville: Abingdon Press, 2007.

Keller, Timothy J. *Center Church: Doing Balanced, Gospel-Centered Ministry in Your Church*. Grand Rapids: Zondervan Publishing House, 2012.

Kimbrough, S. T. *A Song for the Poor: Hymns by Charles Wesley*. New York: General Board of Global Missions, 1997.

Leitch, Ian. *Life Before Death*. Larkspur, CO: Green Acres Press, 2007.

Lewis, C. S. *Mere Christianity*. London: Fontana Books, 1955.

_____. *The Weight of Glory and Other Addresses*. Grand Rapids: William B. Eerdmans Publishing Company, 1949.

Maddox, Randy L. *Responsible Grace: John Wesley's Practical Theology*. Nashville: Kingswood Books, 1994.

Manning, Brennan. *Abba's Child: The Cry of the Heart for Intimate Belonging*. Colorado Springs, CO: Navpress, 1994.

Moule, Handley. *Charles Simeon: Pastor of a Generation*. Fearn, Ross-Shire, Great Britain: Christian Focus, 1997.

Newbegin, Lesslie. *The Gospel in a Pluralist Society*. Grand Rapids: William B. Eerdmans, 1989.

Oden, Thomas C. *Doctrinal Standards in the Wesleyan Tradition*. Grand Rapids: Zondervan, 1988.

_____. *John Wesley's Scriptural Christianity*. Grand Rapids: Zondervan Publishing House, 1994.

Ortberg, John. *The Me I Want to Be: Becoming God's Best Version of You*. Grand Rapids: Zondervan Publishing House, 2009.

Oswalt, John N. *Called to Be Holy: A Biblical Perspective*. Nappanee, Indiana: Francis Asbury Press, 1999.

Outler, Albert C. *John Wesley (A Library of Protestant Thought)*. New York: Oxford University Press, 1964.

_____. *Theology in the Wesleyan Spirit*. Nashville: Discipleship Resources, 1975.

Outler, Albert C., and Richard P. Heitzenrater. *John Wesley's Sermons: An Anthology*. Nashville: Abingdon Press, 1991.

Peters, John L. *Christian Perfection and American Methodism*. Salem, OH: Schmul Publishing Company, 1995.

Phillips, J. B. *The Newborn Christian*. New York: Macmillan, 1978.

Rack, Henry D. *Reasonable Enthusiast: John Wesley and the Rise of Methodism*. Nashville: Abingdon Press, 1989.

Runyon, Theodore. *The New Creation: John Wesley's Theology Today*. Nashville: Abingdon Press, 1998.

Ryle, J. C. *Holiness: Its Nature, Hindrances, Difficulties, and Roots*. Peabody, MA: Hendrickson Publishers, reprint 2007 (1877).

Seamands, Stephen. *Ministry in the Image of God: The Trinitarian Shape of Christian Service*. Downers Grove, IL: InterVarsity Books, 2005.

Swindoll, Charles R. *The Tale of the Tardy Oxcart*. Nashville: Word Publishing, 1998.

Telford, John. *The Life of John Wesley*. New York: Eaton & Mains, 1886.

Thomas, Gary. *Sacred Marriage*. Grand Rapids: Zondervan, 2000.

Tozer, A. W. *That Incredible Christian*. Harp Hill, PA: Wing Spread Publishers, 1964.

Tyerman, Luke. *The Life and Times of the Rev. John Wesley, M.A.* Vols. 1–3, New York: Burt Franklin, 1872.

Vanhoozer, Kevin J. *The Drama of Doctrine*. Louisville, KY: Westminster John Knox Press, 2005.

Willard, Dallas. *The Divine Conspiracy: Rediscovering Our Hidden Life in God*. San Francisco: HarperSanFrancisco, 1998.

_____. *Hearing God: Developing a Conversational Relationship with God*. Downers Grove, IL: InterVarsity Press, 1999.

_____. *Renovation of the Heart: Putting On the Character of Christ.* Colorado Springs, CO: NavPress, 2002.

Williams, Colin W. *John Wesley's Theology Today.* Nashville: Abingdon Press, 1960.

Willimon, William H. *This We Believe: The Core of Wesleyan Faith and Practice.* Nashville: Abingdon Press, 2010.

Witherington, Ben, III. *A Shared Christian Life.* Nashville: Abingdon Press, 2012.

Wright, N. T. *The Last Word: Beyond the Bible Wars to a New Understanding of Scripture.* San Francisco: Harper SanFrancisco, 2005.

_____. *Scripture and the Authority of God.* San Francisco: HarperOne, 2013.

_____. *Simply Christian: Why Christianity Makes Sense.* San Francisco: HarperCollins Publishers, 2006.

Yancey, Philip. *The Jesus I Never Knew.* Grand Rapids: Zondervan Publishing House, 2002.

_____. *What Good Is God: In Search of a Faith That Matters.* New York: FaithWords, 2010.

Yancey, Philip. *What's So Amazing About Grace?* Grand Rapids: Zondervan Publishing House, 1997.

Edited Books

Alexander, Donald L. *Christian Spirituality: Five Views of Sanctification.* Downers Grove, IL: InterVarsity Press, 1988.

Allen Woody, "My Philosophy," *The New Yorker*, December 27, 1969, 23–26.

Green, Joel B., and David F. Watson. *Wesleyans and Reading the Bible as Scripture.* Waco, TX: Baylor University Press, 2012.

Gunter, W. Stephen, et al. *Wesley and the Quadrilateral: Renewing the Conversation.* Nashville: Abingdon Press, 1997

Job, Rueben P., ed. *The United Methodist Hymnal.* Nashville: United Methodist Publishing House, 1989.

Reimann, James, ed., Oswald Chambers. *My Utmost for His Highest: An Updated Edition in Today's Language.* Grand Rapids: Discovery House Publishers, 1992.

Articles/Web Sources

O. Nancy, "The Man on the Bed," *barefootsworld.net*, (July 17, 2001). Barefootsworld.net/aabilld-aa3.html (accessed September 7, 2015).

Rowel, Jeren. *Wesley Center Online*, "Wesley Covenant Service—1998," Wesley.nnu.edu/.../Wesley-covenant-service-1998-jeren-rowel (accessed September 6, 2015).

Seamands, David. Sermon: "Christianizing Our Complexes." Wilmore United Methodist Church, Wilmore, Kentucky.

Skiba, Pete. "Director: Tough Rules Required to Maintain Order." *Albany Herald* 120, no. 35 (September 28, 2012).

Spurgeon, Charles, "The Lover of God's Law Filled With Peace." January 22, 1988. Spurgeongems.org (accessed September 7, 2015).

Watson, David. *Cross Way*, "Great Anglican Divines (5) John Pearson—Bishop of Chester, 1613–1668," Winter 1986, no. 23.

Index of Names

Hammerschold, Dag, 125
Harper, Steve, 128–129
Heitzenrater, Richard, xxiii, 64, 65,
    113, 114, 120
Hervey, James, 3
Heston, Charlton, 55
Homer, 9
Homilies, 17
Horace, 9

Ignatius, 16
Iliad, 9
Izzard, Eddie, 45

Job, Bishop Reuben, 64, 65
Johnson, Samuel, 9
John the Baptist, 51
John (J. R.), 87
Jones, E. Stanley, 105

Karen, 87
Keller, Tim, 103
Kessler, Major General Jim, xi
King George ii, 101
Kings Bay Naval Submarine base, xvi

Lackington, James, 131–132
Leitch, Ian, 39
Lewis, C. S., 60, 70, 71, 85, 105, 109,
    120
Lincoln, Abraham, 109
Locke, John, 2
Luther, Martin, 19, 43, 62, 82

Maddox, Randy, 22, 28, 29, 36, 86
March, Miss, 132
Marston, V. Paul, 119
Marx, Karl, 42
Mennenger, Karl, 101
Mere Christianity, 60
Message, The, 119
Middleton, Conyers, 16
Milton, John, 9

*Nature, Design, and General Rule of the
    United Societies, The*, 65
Newton, Isaac, 9

Newton, John, 2, 34
Noah, 112

Oden, Thomas, 16, 46, 53
Origen, 8, 16
Ortberg, John, 45
Outler, Albert C., xxi, 8, 9, 102, 134
Ovid, 9

Pearson, Bishop John, 17
Pelagius, 45
Peters, John, 126
Phillips, J. B., 97, 107
Pilgrim's Progress, 5
*Plain Account of Genuine Christianity,
    A*, xxii, 80
Plato, 9

Rack, Henry, 9, 100
*Renewal of the Heart is The Mission of
    the Church, The*, 39
Responsible Grace, 28
Runyon, Theodore, 37
Russell H., 76–78
Ryle, J. C., 42

Sanhedrin, 97
Seven Habits of Highly Effective People,
    80
Shakespeare. William, 9
Shared Christian Life, A, 118
Simeon, Charles, xxii
Sinatra, Frank, 134
Smith, Bob, 122
Smith, John, 21, 22, 34, 89
Society For Promoting Christian
    Knowledge, 113
Spangenburg, August, 82
Spurgeon, Charles, 3
Sunee, 87
*Survey of the Wisdom of God in Cre-
    ation, A*, 9

Telford, John, 8
Tertullian, 16
Thackery, William M., 101
*Three Simple Rules: A Wesleyan Way of
    Living*, 64

Index of Subjects

responsible grace, 28, 31, 32, 71, 74
Reveal Spiritual Life Survey, xiii

sanctification, 4, 36, 60, 95, 97–99,
    100, 112, 122, 123, 134
sanctifying grace, 33, 71, 83, 85, 86,
    95, 96, 127
scripture, 1–5, 10, 14, 16, 19, 24, 39,
    43, 44, 55, 92
societies, 65, 66, 114, 119
sovereign grace, 29

spiritual senses, 15
stillness, 35
tempers, 74, 107, 128
therapeutic emphasis, 29
tradition, 14, 16–19, 23, 24, 39, 43

Willow Creek Community Church, xiii
witness of the Spirit, 85, 89, 90, 91
"works meet for repentance," 61–63,
    65, 67

Made in the USA
Middletown, DE
13 October 2022

12653988R00113